Vege-

Ariya Netjoy Presents:

VEGANIZED

ASIAN VEGAN COOKING

Buddha's Way

BE GOOD AND KIND TO ALL LIVING BEINGS

PRACTICE IT

BUDDHA'S WAY

Asian Vegan Bundle Includes:

Vietnam Vegan

Thai Restaurant Recipes

Chinese Healthy Cooking

Filipino Vegan Feast

Vege-Thai-Rian

Ariya Netjoy Presents:

VEGANIZED

VIETNAM VEGAN

Buddha's Way

BE GOOD AND KIND TO ALL LIVING BEINGS

PRACTICE IT

Copyrights 2017 All rights reserved © Ariya Netjoy

No part of this publication or the information in it may be quoted from or reproduced in any form by means such as printing, scanning, photocopying, or otherwise without prior written permission of the copyright holder.

Sunny Thai Publishing

Terms of Use Disclaimer Efforts have been made to ensure that the information in this book is accurate. However, the author and the publisher do not hold any responsibility for errors, omissions, or contrary interpretation of the subject matter herein. The recipes provided in this book are for informational purposes only and are not intended to provide dietary advice. A medical practitioner should be consulted for dietary advice. Additionally, recipe cooking times may require adjustment depending on age and quality of appliances and tools. Readers are urged to take all needed precautions to ensure ingredients are fully cooked to avoid the dangers of foodborne illnesses. The author and publisher do not take any responsibility for any consequences that may result due to following the instructions provided in this book.

Thank you for being a loyal reader and friend. As a reward, we would like to bring even more delicious vegan and vegetarian dishes into your life, FREE! All you have to do, is sign up with your email and you are set. Everything is free and full of fun so come on and eat with us! Click the blue mail above. Available on the Kindle version.

Table of Contents

Introduction
Stir-Fry Green Beans with Potatoes
Stir-Fried Mushrooms Vietnamese Style
Vietnamese Avocado Dessert
Red Sticky Rice (Xoi Gac)
Stir-Fry Water Spinach with Mushrooms
Vietnamese Vegan Noodles Soup (Vietnamese Vegetarian Pho)
Cauliflower Couscous Vietnamese Style
(Che Bap) Vietnamese Corn with Sticky Rice
Stir-Fry Tofu and Bean Sprouts
Stir-Fried Bok choy
Tamarind and Pineapple Soup with Tofu
Mixed Fruits with Coconut Milk
Fried Tofu with Sweet and Sour Sauce (Dau Hu Sot Chua Ngot)
Taro Soup Vietnamese Style
Eggplant with Tofu Vietnamese Style
Vietnamese Vegetarian Steamed Dumplings
Vietnamese Green papaya with Carrot Salad
Vietnamese Stir-Fried Mixed Vegetables
Pumpkin Soup Vietnamese Style
Vietnamese Vegan Rice
Vietnamese Watermelon Jelly
Tofu in Tomato Sauce
Water Spinach with Garlic Sauce
Vietnamese Sesame Balls (Banh Ran or Banh Cam)
Vietnamese Rice Porridge
Vietnamese Mung Beans Sweet Dessert
Carrot and Daikon Pickles Vietnamese Style
Hot and Spicy Tofu with Lemongrass Sauce
Tofu with Broccoli in Sweet and Spicy Almond Sauce

Scallion Cake Vietnamese Style
Vietnamese Vegan Spring Rolls
Caramelized Tofu Vietnamese Style
Vietnamese Vegan Banh Mi
Longan and Lotus Seed Sweet Soup
Vietnamese Vegan Crepes
Vietnamese Mixed Vegetable Salad
Tofu Noodle Soup with Broccoli and Bean Sprouts
Red Bean Sweet Soup Vietnamese Style
Vietnamese Pomelo Sweet Soup
Cucumber Salad Vietnamese Style
Chayote Stir-Fry Recipe
Banana with Coconut Milk Vietnamese Dessert
Vietnamese Spinach Soup with Tofu
Stir-Fried Chayote with Broccoli
Vietnamese Kohlrabi Salad
Stir-Fried Bamboo Shoots with Tofu in Ginger Sauce
Black Bean Sweet Vietnamese Dessert
Vietnamese Peanut Sticky Rice (Xoi Lac)
Vietnamese Colorful Rice Cake
Sour Mushroom Soup Vietnamese Style

Introduction

If you are looking for healthy and exquisite vegetarian recipes, then you are on the right cookbook.

Vietnamese cuisine is a mixture of both Asian and Western culture. In the past, Asian countries like China, Malaysia, Thailand, brought different ingredients in Vietnam. The use of coconut milk, soy sauce and chili was then incorporated in Vietnamese cooking. Later on, Western countries brought the use of tomatoes, cakes, and bread in the country. France has the greatest influence in Vietnamese cooking and in the present, Vietnamese has popularized the use of Baguette, a French vegan bread.

Another unique identity of Vietnamese cuisine is the used of herbs. Common herbs in cooking are mint, basil, and coriander. Health is a priority in Vietnamese cuisine specifically for vegetarian recipes. This is due to the doctrines followed by the majority of Buddhist people in Vietnam.

In this cookbook, you will learn different ways of cooking soup, rice cakes and vegetable dishes that are popular in Vietnam. Included in the cookbook are the health benefits provided by different herbs and common vegetables in Vietnamese vegan cooking.

Stir-Fry Green Beans with Potatoes

Ingredients:

- 2 large potatoes (cut into strips)
- 1 cup green beans (cut into strips)
- 2 tablespoon vegetable oil
- ½ cup vegetable stock
- 2 teaspoon sesame seeds
- 1 teaspoon pepper
- 1 teaspoon salt
- 4 cloves garlic (minced)
-

Utensils Needed:

- Frying pan
- Spatula
- Cleaver
- Chopping board
- Mandoline (for shredding vegetables)

Directions:

Wash 2 large potatoes with water and then peel. Remove husk of garlic and then mince using a cleaver. Cut the potatoes into halves then cut into strips using a mandoline. Now, wash green beans and cut into strips diagonally. Set aside.

In a frying pan, put 2 tablespoons of vegetable oil. Add garlic and sauté until it turns brown. Put shredded potatoes into the pan and stir-fry for about 5 minutes. Pour ½ cup of vegetable stock into the pan and cover. Bring to simmer, then add the green beans when the broth is reduced. Stir-fry until vegetables are tender. Sprinkle with salt and pepper. Make sure to stir frequently to combine all ingredients. Serve warm with sesame seeds on top. Good for 4-5 persons.

Health Tips:

- Green beans contain ample amount of flavonoids. According to many studies, flavonoids boost your immune system and prevents free radical damage that causes cancer. Eating green beans can lower your risk of various diseases due to the flavonoids ability to enhance the immune system of the body.

Stir-Fried Mushrooms Vietnamese Style

Ingredients:

- 400 grams king oyster mushrooms (cut into medium sizes)
- ¼ cup vegetable broth
- 2 red chili (minced)
- 2 cloves garlic (minced)
- 1 medium onion (cut into small pieces)
- 2 tablespoon light soy sauce
- 2 tablespoon vegetable oil
- 1 teaspoon sugar
- 1 teaspoon salt
- 2 teaspoon pineapple juice
- ½ teaspoon pepper
- 2 teaspoon chopped cilantro

Utensils Needed:

- Wok
- Spatula
- Cleaver
- Chopping board

Directions:

Wash and drain king oyster mushrooms. Remove the roots and slice into medium sizes. Prepare garlic, red chili, and onions. Rinse with water and mince. Save for later use.

Add 2 tablespoon of vegetable oil in a wok. Heat oil over medium flame and add the minced garlic, onions and red chili. Sauté until onion turns translucent. Put 400 grams of sliced mushroom into the wok and stir-fry until tender. Add ¼ cup of vegetable broth and let it simmer. When the broth is simmering, add 2 tablespoons of light soy sauce, 1 teaspoon of sugar, and 2 teaspoons of pineapple juice. Stir all ingredients and add salt and pepper. Cook for another 2 minutes and then sprinkle with chopped cilantro. Serve warm to 5-6 persons.

Health Tips:

- King Oyster Mushroom is the biggest among the oyster mushroom family. Like all the mushroom species, it acts as a powerful anti-bacterial agent in the body and helps prevent diseases. If you include mushrooms in your meals, your body is safe from acquiring viruses or bacteria.

Vietnamese Avocado Dessert

Ingredients:

- 2 large Avocado (ripe)
- 1 and ½ cup ice (crushed)
- 4 tablespoons maple syrup
- 1 cup coconut or almond milk
- Small chunks of avocado (garnish)

Utensils Needed:

- Blender
- Ice smasher
- Blender spoon/spatula
- Kitchen Knife
- Chopping board

Directions:

Rinse avocado with water and cut in the center lengthwise. Remove the seed and peel the skin. Chop the avocado flesh into small pieces and set aside.

Get cubed ice and crush using an ice smasher or ice grinder. Save for later use.

Prepare a blender. Put almond milk or coconut milk, maple syrup, and chopped avocados into the blender. Blend until coarsely smooth.

In a tall glass or deep bowl, put crushed ice first and then followed by avocado mixture. Serve with small chunks of avocado on top. Good for 2-3 persons.

Health Tips:

- Avocados are widely known as a superfood. It con-

tains a lot of vitamins and minerals that keep your body healthy and strong. Loaded with potassium, fiber, monounsaturated fats, which are good for your heart, DNA cells and your gastrointestinal system.
- A good alternative for sugar is maple syrup. It has polyphenols that can reduce inflammation in the body. If you're suffering from asthma, which is an inflammation of the airway, maple syrup can help prevent an asthma attack. Its anti-inflammatory effect can also help heal wound faster.

Red Sticky Rice (Xoi Gac)

Ingredients:

- 1 kg glutinous rice
- 2 tablespoon white wine
- 500 grams gac paste
- 1 tablespoon salt
- 1 and ½ cup sugar
- 1 can of coconut milk

Utensils Needed:

- Chopsticks
- Steamer
- Clear disposable gloves
- Large mixing bowl
- Molds or small bowls

Directions:

Rinse and drain glutinous rice with water 4 to 5 times. Add gac paste into the drained glutinous rice. Use clear disposable gloves to combine gac paste and rice. This will prevent the rice from sticking in your hands. Mix in 1 tablespoon of salt and 2 tablespoons of white wine. Let it stand for an hour or two.

Prepare a steamer, and put the mixture of glutinous rice into the steamer. Cook for about 30 minutes. Make sure to stir using chopsticks to cook the rice evenly. Add 1 and ½-cup sugar and slowly add milk into the rice cake. Stir continuously while adding the milk and sugar. Steam for another 5-7 minutes. After cooking, transfer to small molds or bowls. Serve warm to 6-8 persons.

Health Tips:

- Gac fruit or baby jackfruit is commonly used in Vietnam during important ceremonies or celebration. It has a mild mushy taste, which is good for rice cakes. Gac fruit is packed with nutrients and minerals that are good for your body. If you want your vision to stay clear and healthy, you should eat gac fruit because it has more beta-carotene and lycopene than tomatoes and carrots.

Stir-Fry Water Spinach with Mushrooms

Ingredients:

- 500 grams water spinach (chopped)
- 400 grams mushrooms (cut into halves)
- 2 tablespoons spring onions (chopped)
- 1 tablespoon sesame seeds
- 3 cloves garlic (minced)
- 2 tablespoon light soy sauce
- ¼ cup vegetable broth
- 2 teaspoon corn starch
- 4 garlic cloves
- 1 medium onion (minced)
- 2 tablespoon sesame oil
- 1 teaspoon pepper

Utensils Needed:

- Wok
- Wooden spatula
- Cleaver
- Chopping board

Directions:

Wash water spinach and mushrooms with water and pat to dry. Remove dried and yellowish leaves from the water spinach. Snap off the hard stem end of the water spinach and cut off the stems of the mushrooms. Cut mushroom caps into halves and chop water spinach into medium sizes. Prepare onion, spring onions and garlic. Mince and set aside.

In a wok, add 2 tablespoons of sesame oil. Once the oil is hot, add garlic and onion. Stir-fry until garlic is brown or onion is transparent. Put mushrooms first and sauté for about 3 minutes, and then add the water spinach. Pour ¼ cup of vegetable stock, add 2 teaspoons of cornstarch and mix well.

Bring to simmer. When sauce thickens, add 2 tablespoons of light soy sauce and sprinkle with pepper. Stir frequently. Season with sesame seeds and minced spring onions. Serve with rice to 5-6 persons.

Health Tips:

- Do you want to have a smooth and healthy skin? Water spinach can help remove acne or pimples. Eating this vegetable can make your skin glow. It helps in removing toxins out of the body and thus keeping your skin healthy and smooth.

Vietnamese Vegan Noodles Soup (Vietnamese Vegetarian Pho)

Ingredients:

- 250 grams rice noodles
- 100 grams mushrooms (cut into halves)
- 5 cups water
- 3 cups vegetable stock
- 3 tablespoons spring onions (chopped)
- 2 tablespoons cilantro (coarsely chopped)
- 4 pieces lime wedge (garnish)
- 3 tablespoon tamari sauce
- 1 tablespoon white vinegar
- 1 cinnamon stick
- 1 clove
- 2 star anise
- 2 garlic cloves (minced)
- 1 large onion (minced)
- 3 inch ginger (grated)

Ingredients:

- Large pot
- Saucepan
- Ladle
- Cleaver
- Chopping board
- Strainer

Directions:

Prepare all ingredients. Rinse all vegetables with water and pat to dry. Cut mushroom caps into halves, mince onion and garlic, grate the ginger and chop cilantro and spring onions. Save for later use.

Prepare a saucepan over medium heat. Add 2-star anise, 1 cinnamon stick, and 1 clove into the saucepan. Cook until aroma becomes fragrant. Now, pour 4 cups of vegetable stock, 3 tablespoons of tamari sauce and 1 tablespoon of white vinegar into the saucepan. Add ginger, onion, and garlic. Stir to combine all ingredients and cover the pan. Lower the flame and bring to simmer. Cook for 20 minutes.

While cooking the soup, you can prepare your rice noodles. Cook rice noodles in a pot of boiling water until it becomes slightly tender. Do not overcook. Strain the noodles and set aside.

Now prepare 4 bowls and transfer noodles in each bowl. Pour soup into each bowl just enough to soak the noodles. Add spring onions, a slice of lime wedge and cilantro in each bowl. Serve hot to 4 persons.

Health Tips:

- If you want to enhance the flavor of different recipes, and you want to boost your immune system too, you should add star anise in your dish. It works as an antioxidant, helping your body to fight against free radical damage that can cause cancer.

Cauliflower Couscous Vietnamese Style

Ingredients:

- 1 big cauliflower head (cut into small florets)
- 1 large yellow bell pepper (cubed)
- 1 large red bell pepper (cubed)
- 1 medium size carrot (cubed)
- 1 medium size cucumber (diced)
- 1 large tomato (diced)
- ½ bunch parsley (minced)
- 3 tablespoon lime juice
- 1 tablespoon lime zest
- 2 tablespoon olive oil
- 1 teaspoon salt
- ½ teaspoon pepper

Utensils Needed:

- Food processor or Blender
- Kitchen Knife or Cleaver
- Chopping board
- Mixing bowl
- Small wooden spatula
- Large pot with water (for boiling the cauliflower)
- Strainer

Directions:

Prepare 1 large cauliflower head and soak in cold water to remove the dirt. Pat to dry and then cut into small florets. Wash all the other vegetables with running water and cut into cubes.

Cook cauliflower florets in a pot of boiling water for 2-3 minutes and then drain. Transfer the cooked florets in a bowl of cold water and let it sit for 3 minutes. Dry with a clean cloth and put florets in a blender. Blend florets until it turns roughly smooth.

Get a mixing bowl and pour cauliflower couscous into it. Mix all the other cubed vegetables into the bowl. Stir using a wooden spatula. Add 3 tablespoon of lime juice and a tablespoon of lime zest into the bowl. Sprinkle with salt and pepper, then combine all ingredients well. Good for 3-4 persons.

Health Tips:

- One of the best vegetables to eat after exercising is cauliflower. It contains potassium, a major electrolyte that helps maintain pH level in the body. When you lack potassium, you can experience leg cramps or muscle strain. Making a dish out of cauliflower after your workout will prevent you from any muscle cramps.

(Che Bap) Vietnamese Corn with Sticky Rice

Ingredients:

- 500 grams sweet corn kernels
- 1 cup coconut milk
- ¼ cup sticky rice
- 4 cups water
- 4 tablespoon tapioca pearls
- 1 tablespoon maple syrup
- 6 tablespoon sugar
- 1/3 cup coconut cream
- ½ teaspoon salt

Utensils Needed:

- Saucepan
- pot
- Ladle
- Bowls

Directions:

Prepare all ingredients for corn soup. Get a pot and pour 4 cups of water. Turn stove on medium flame and add tapioca pearls. Cover the pot and bring to simmer. Cook for about 15 minutes until pearls become transparent. Now, add the glutinous rice, and stir continuously while cooking. Slowly add corn kernels and stir frequently. Add 6 tablespoons of sugar and 1/3 cup of coconut cream and then mix the mixture thoroughly. Sprinkle half a teaspoon of salt. Cook for another 5-7 minutes. Stir frequently. When the soup thickens, transfer it to small bowls. Save for later use.

In a saucepan, pour coconut milk and 1 tablespoon of maple syrup. Cover the pan and let it simmer for 3-4 minutes. Occasionally stir the mixture while cooking. Pour the coconut mixture into each bowl of glutinous corn. Serve hot to 4-6 persons.

Health Tips:
- Corn is packed with two minerals. These are Phosphorus and Magnesium. These minerals can help your bones become stronger and maintain a normal heart and kidney function.

BUDDHA'S WAY

Stir-Fry Tofu and Bean Sprouts

Ingredients:

- 500 grams tofu (cubed)
- 400 grams bean sprouts (trimmed)
- 1 large red bell pepper (julienned)
- 1 tablespoon chopped basil leaves
- 1 large onion (chopped)
- 2 tablespoon light soy sauce
- A pinch of salt
- 3 tablespoon vegetable oil

Utensils:

- Frying pan
- Spatula
- Chopping board
- Cleaver

Directions:

Wash vegetables and tofu with water. Dry the vegetables by using a clean cloth. Drain excess water from tofu by pressing. Slice each vegetable into your desired shape and cut tofu into cubes. Set aside.

Prepare a frying pan and add 3 tablespoons vegetable oil. Stir-fry tofu until golden on both sides. Add bean sprouts, sliced red bell peppers, and onion into the frying pan. Stir for about 2-3 minutes. Now, pour 2 tablespoons of light soy sauce and season with a dash of salt. Continue stirring for another minute until all ingredients are well combined. Sprinkle with chopped basil leaves and serve warm to 4 persons.

Health Tips:

- Basil has antibacterial properties, which is beneficial

for your immune system to fight against diseases. According to recent studies, basil leaves can help your body against resistant bacteria that can't be cured by modern medicines.

Stir-Fried Bok choy

Ingredients:

- 500 grams Bok choy (chopped)
- 2 garlic cloves (minced)
- ½ teaspoon black pepper
- 1 teaspoon salt
- 1 tablespoon light soy sauce
- ¼ cup vegetable stock
- 2 teaspoon sesame seeds
- 2 tablespoon olive oil

Utensils Needed:

- Frying pan or wok
- Spatula
- Kitchen knife
- Chopping board

Directions:

Wash Bok choy with cold running water. Cut off the hard stalk end to separate leaves and then chop into medium sizes. Mince 2 cloves of garlic and set aside.

Heat 2 tablespoons of olive oil in a wok or frying pan. Sauté minced garlic and cook until it turns brown. Add 500 grams chopped Bok choy into the wok. Stir-fry until tender. Pour ¼ cup of vegetable stock into the wok and add a tablespoon of light soy sauce. Season with sesame seeds, black pepper and salt. Toss all ingredients together and cook for another 2-3 minutes. Serve warm to 4 persons.

Health Tips:

- If you want to lose fats, you should eat some Bok Choy. This vegetable is very low in calories. You don't need to worry eating a lot of it since it also packed with minerals and anti-oxidants that are good for the cells in your body.

Tamarind and Pineapple Soup with Tofu

Ingredients:

- 500 grams tofu (cubed)
- 350 grams rice noodles
- 5 cups of water
- 2 cups of vegetable stock
- 1 can pineapple chunk
- 4 large tomatoes (chopped)
- 3 tablespoon tamarind extract
- 3 tablespoon sugar
- 1 stalk lemon grass
- 2 tablespoon olive oil
- A bunch of spring onions (chopped)
- 2 teaspoon chili paste
- 1 teaspoon salt

Utensils Needed:

- Strainer
- Pot
- Soup bowls
- Kitchen knife
- Chopping board
- Mortar and pestle
- Wooden spatula
- ladle

Directions:

Cook 350 grams of rice noodles in a pot of boiling water until just tender. Drain and transfer to small soup bowls. Set aside.

Get a mortar and pestle and bruise 1 stalk of lemon grass. Add 3 tablespoons of tamarind extract, 2-teaspoon chili paste and 3-tablespoon sugar. Mix using a small wooden spatula and set aside.

Now prepare your tamarind and pineapple soup. In a pot over medium flame, add 2 tablespoons of olive oil. Once the oil is shimmering, sauté onion until translucent. Add cubed tofu and stir-fry until slightly brown on both sides. Pour 5 cups of water and 2 cups of vegetable stock into the pot. Mix in the prepared tamarind mixture and 1 can of pineapple chunks. Cover the pot and bring to a boil. Make sure to stir occasionally while cooking. Add chopped tomatoes and reduce the heat. Simmer for 5-10 minutes and then sprinkle with a teaspoon of salt.

Pour tamarind soup over the bowls of rice noodles. Serve with chopped spring onions. Good for 5 persons.

Health Tips:
- Lemongrass can treat abdominal problems like constipation, stomach cramps or indigestion. In the past, it has always been used as a traditional remedy for many gastrointestinal problems, especially among Asian countries. Lemongrass has a compound called Citral, which is responsible for proper digestion.
- Pineapple is a rich source of fiber. Fiber aids in good digestion and prevent you from having any constipation. Combining pineapple and lemongrass in a dish guarantees healthier tummy.

Mixed Fruits with Coconut Milk

Ingredients:

- 1 can of coconut milk
- ½ cup coconut cream
- 1 can of lychees
- 1 can of coconut jelly
- ½ can pineapple chunks
- 1 cup cooked gelatin (diced)
- 3 tablespoon sugar

Utensils Needed:

- Saucepan
- Ladle
- Mixing bowl
- Wooden spatula
- Kitchen knife
- Chopping board

Directions:

In a saucepan, heat a can of coconut milk, ½ cup of coconut cream and 3 tablespoons of sugar. Simmer for 5-7 minutes while stirring to dissolve the sugar completely. Set aside to cool.

Prepare a mixing bowl. Combine lychees, pineapple chunks, cooked and diced gelatin, and coconut jelly in the bowl. Include the syrup of lychees, pineapple chunks and coconut jelly. Now, pour the cooled coconut mixture into the bowl and mix using a wooden spatula. Put inside the refrigerator for a couple of hours. Serve chilled to 3-4 persons.

Health Tips:

- Lychees contain copper, an important mineral in red blood cell production apart from Iron. Eating lychees can improve your blood circulation.

Fried Tofu with Sweet and Sour Sauce (Dau Hu Sot Chua Ngot)

Ingredients:

- 500 grams tofu (diced)
- 3 tablespoon olive oil
- 1 bunch of spring onions (chopped)
- 3 tablespoon vegetable stock
- 1 tablespoon light soy sauce
- 2 tablespoon maple syrup
- 2 tablespoon tamarind paste
- 1 teaspoon chili paste
- 1 teaspoon salt

Utensils Needed:

- Spatula
- Wok or frying pan
- Cleaver
- Chopping board
- Mixing bowl
- Small wooden spatula

Directions:

Rinse and drain 500 grams tofu. Cut tofu into cubes and set aside. Chop spring onions and save for garnish.

Prepare a small mixing bowl for the sweet and sour sauce. Combine 1 tablespoon of light soy sauce, 2 tablespoons of maple syrup and tamarind paste in the bowl. Mix using a wooden spatula. Add chili paste and stir well.

In a wok, heat 3 tablespoons of olive oil. Once the oil is hot, stir-fry cubed tofu until golden on both sides. Pour the sweet and sour sauce into the wok and mix carefully with the fried tofu. Cook for about 3-4 minutes over low heat. Serve warm with rice to 4-6 persons.

Health Tips:

- Tofu consumption can decrease cholesterol level in the body. It absorbs fat and minimizes cardiovascular problems like heart attack brought by accumulation of plaques in the blood vessels.

Taro Soup Vietnamese Style

Ingredients:

- 500 grams taro (peeled and chopped)
- 5 cups vegetable stock
- 200 grams tofu (diced)
- ½ cup peanuts
- 2 tablespoon cilantro (chopped)
- 2 tablespoon chopped spring onions
- 1 teaspoon salt
- ½ teaspoon pepper
- 2 garlic cloves (chopped)
- 3 tablespoon vegetable oil
- 1 tablespoon light soy sauce

Utensils Needed:

- Pot
- Ladle
- Cleaver
- Chopping board
- Frying pan
- Spatula
- Strainer
- saucepan

Directions:

Soak peanuts in water for a couple of hours. Drain and then boil in a saucepan. Let it cool and set aside.

Rinse and drain tofu. Slice into cubes. Get a frying pan and add 3 tablespoons of vegetable oil. Fry tofu until it turns brown on both sides. Transfer to a plate with paper towel to remove excess oil. Save for later use.

Wash taro with water and peel the skin. Cut into bite size pieces and boil in a pot of water. Cook until tender and then drain the taro using a strainer. Pour 5 cups of vegetable stock into the pot. Add boiled peanuts and fried tofu. Stir and cover the pot. Simmer for 5 minutes. Now, add cooked taro, 1 teaspoon of salt, 1 tablespoon of light soy sauce and half a teaspoon of pepper. Sprinkle with cilantro and spring onions. Mix all ingredients well. Cook for another 5-7 minutes until taro becomes soft. Good for 6-7 persons.

Health Benefits:

- Taro contains both Vitamin A and Vitamin E. Two vitamins that are responsible for keeping your skin healthy and smooth. Vitamin A is also good for your vision and Vitamin E improves overall cell function.
- Peanuts have ample amounts of Vitamin B, like niacin, thiamin, and folate. These are essential in maintaining the overall function of the heart, and nervous system.

Eggplant with Tofu Vietnamese Style

Ingredients:

- 500 grams tofu (cubed)
- 1 large eggplant (sliced)
- 2 garlic cloves (minced)
- 1 teaspoon chili paste
- 2 inches ginger (minced)
- 1 teaspoon agave nectar
- ½ teaspoon black pepper
- 2 teaspoons sesame seeds
- 1 tablespoon tamari sauce
- 4 tablespoon vegetable oil
- 1 teaspoon salt
- 2 tablespoon vegetable stock
- 2 teaspoon cornstarch
- 2 tablespoon chopped spring onions

Utensils Needed:

- Wok
- Spatula
- Cleaver
- Chopping board

Directions:

Wash eggplant and garlic with water. Remove the husk of garlic cloves and then mince. Slice eggplants into cubes. Rinse tofu with water and drain excess fluids by pressing. Cut tofu into cubes and then set aside.

Pour 4 tablespoons of vegetable oil in a wok. Turn your stove on medium flame. Once the oil is hot and shimmering, add garlic. Sauté until golden. Now, add cubed tofu and stir-fry until slightly brown on both sides. Mix in the eggplants and stir-fry until crisp. Add 1 tablespoon of tamari sauce, 2 tablespoons of vegetable stock and 1 teaspoon of agave nectar into the wok. Toss all ingredients to coat tofu and eggplants well with the sauce. Add chili paste and cornstarch into the pot. Stir until cornstarch dissolves completely into the sauce. Cover the wok and let it simmer for 3 minutes. Sprinkle with salt and black pepper. Mix well. Add chopped spring onions and sesame seeds. Good for 5 persons.

Health Tips:
- Eggplant can help enhance your cognitive abilities. It prevents you from getting any diseases related to poor memory, like dementia or Alzheimer's disease.

Vietnamese Vegetarian Steamed Dumplings

Ingredients:

- 1/2 cup coarsely grated carrots
- 30 pieces vegan wonton wrappers
- ¼ cup carrots (minced)
- ¼ cup cabbage (shredded)
- ¼ cup red bell pepper (minced)
- 1 tablespoon tamari sauce
- 1 tablespoon hoisin sauce
- 1 teaspoon salt
- 1 teaspoon pepper
- 1 tablespoon parsley
- 1 teaspoon Vietnamese mint
- 1 large onion (minced)
- 2 inch ginger (minced)

Utensils Needed:

- Steamer
- Baking sheet or baking pan
- Cleaver
- Chopping board
- Wok
- Spatula
- bowl

Directions:

Prepare all your vegetables and wash with water. Mince all ingredients or cut into small pieces. Now, get a wok and add 2 tablespoons of vegetable oil. Add minced ginger, onion, carrots, cabbage, and red bell pepper into the wok. Stir-fry for 2-3 minutes and then add hoisin sauce, tamari sauce, Vietnamese mint, and parsley. Continue mixing all ingredients and then season with salt and pepper. Transfer in a bowl and let it cool.

Place a baking sheet or baking pan on your kitchen table. Layer vegan wonton wrappers on the baking sheet. Wet all sides with water and put a tablespoon of mixed vegetables in the center of the wrapper. Shape as desired. Now, layer the dumplings in a steamer and cook for 10-11 minutes. Serve warm to 6-7 persons.

Health Benefits:

- Carrots contain a high amount of beta-carotene. It acts as an anti-oxidant and delays aging process of the cells in the body. If you want to stay younger, you should add carrots in your recipes.

Vietnamese Green papaya with Carrot Salad

Ingredients:

- 500 grams green papaya (julienned)
- 350 grams carrots (cut into thin strips)
- 1 tablespoon Vietnamese mint
- 1 tablespoon cilantro
- 1 tablespoon basil leaves
- 1 tablespoon shallots (minced)
- 2 tablespoon apple cider vinegar
- 2 tablespoon light soy sauce
- 1 tablespoon lime zest
- 1 tablespoon maple syrup
- 1 teaspoon salt
- ½ teaspoon black pepper

Utensils Needed:

- Large mixing bowl
- 2 small wooden spatula (for mixing ingredients)
- Pot of water
- Strainer
- mandoline

Directions:

Wash carrots and papaya with water and then remove the skin. Prepare a pot of boiling water. Cook papaya and carrots for about 2-3 minutes. Drain and let it cool.

Rinse onions, mint, cilantro and basil with water and then cut into the desired shape. Cut cooked papaya and carrots using a mandoline. Now, get a large mixing bowl, combine chopped herbs and vegetables into the bowl. Pour light soy sauce, apple cider vinegar, and maple syrup into the bowl. Toss all ingredients well by using two wooden spoons or spatula. Add 1 tablespoon of lime zest and sprinkle with salt and pepper. Mix thoroughly. Put in the refrigerator for an hour and serve chilled to 3-4 persons.

Health Tips:

- If you want something sweet but you don't want to get your blood sugar level increased, then you should be eating papayas. Papaya is good for diabetics. It is low in sugar and rich in fiber.

Vietnamese Stir-Fried Mixed Vegetables

Ingredients:

- 1 head cauliflower (cut into florets)
- 1 medium size carrots (chopped)
- 300 grams cabbage (chopped)
- 2-3 birds eye chili (chopped)
- ½ cup of vegetable stock
- 2 teaspoon cornstarch
- 1 tablespoon light soy sauce
- 2 tablespoon olive oil
- 1 teaspoon black pepper
- 1 large onion (minced)

Utensils Needed:

- Wok or frying pan
- Spatula
- Chopping board
- Kitchen knife

Directions:

Wash cabbage, cauliflower, onion, bird's eye chili and carrots with cold running water. Cut cauliflower into small florets. Chop carrots, cabbage and bird's eye chili into medium sizes. Remove the skin of onion and mince. Save everything for later use.

In a wok over medium heat, add 2 tablespoons of olive oil. Sauté onion until translucent. Add cauliflower florets, cabbage, carrots into the wok. Stir-fry until tender. Mix in the chopped bird's eye chili and pour half a cup of vegetable stock. Stir all ingredients and cover the wok. Let it simmer for 3-5 minutes. Now, add 1 tablespoon of light soy sauce and 2 teaspoon of cornstarch. Season with salt and black pepper. Mix well. Cook until sauce thickens. Stir occasionally to avoid burning the vegetables. Serve warm with rice to 4-5 persons.

Health Tips:

- Bird's eye chili helps reduce weight. It increases your body's metabolism thus helping you to lose some weight. Adding this to your recipe will not just spice up the dish but also spice up your body.

Pumpkin Soup Vietnamese Style

Ingredients:

- 350 grams pumpkin (diced)
- 1 tablespoon light soy sauce
- 1 tablespoon vegetable oil
- 2 garlic cloves (chopped)
- 2 inches ginger (chopped)
- 2 tablespoon spring onions (chopped)
- 1 tablespoon coriander (chopped)
- ½ cup glutinous rice
- 3 tablespoon sugar
- 1 teaspoon salt
- ½ teaspoon pepper
- 3 cups water
- 2 cups vegetable stock

Utensils Needed:

- Pot
- Ladle
- Cleaver
- Chopping board

Directions:

Wash pumpkin with water and remove the skin. Cut into small cubes. Rinse spring onions, garlic, coriander and garlic with water. Chop all vegetables and herbs and then save for later use.

In a pot, pour 3 cups of water and 2 cups of vegetable stock. Turn stove on medium flame and add cubed pumpkin and ½-cup glutinous rice. Stir well and cover the pot. Cook until pumpkin is soft. Frequently stir while cooking to avoid the rice from sticking at the bottom of the pot. Now, add chopped garlic and ginger, then put 1 tablespoon of light soy sauce and dissolve 3 tablespoons of sugar into the pot. Mix everything well. Cover the pot and cook for another 5-7 minutes. Season with salt and pepper. Wait until the soup thickens before serving. Add chopped spring onions and coriander for garnish. Serve hot to 5-6 persons.

Health Tips:

- Pumpkin has a unique natural compound called Phytosterol, which aids in reducing the bad cholesterol in the body. Eating pumpkin will prevent you from getting any serious problem brought by too much bad cholesterol level in the body.

Vietnamese Vegan Rice

Ingredients:

- 4 cups cooked rice
- 3 cloves garlic (minced)
- 1 bunch spring onions (chopped)
- 1 small carrot (cut into small cubes)
- 1 red bell pepper (cut into small cubes)
- 3 tablespoon vegetable oil
- ½ teaspoon chili powder
- 1 teaspoon black pepper
- 1 teaspoon salt
- 1 tablespoon light soy sauce
- 1 medium size onion (minced)
- A bunch of celery (chopped)

Utensils Needed:

- Wok
- Spatula
- Chopping board
- Kitchen knife
- Kitchen disposable gloves

Directions:

Prepare 4 cups of cooked rice. Make sure to separate each grain of rice. Wear kitchen disposable gloves and manually separate grains of rice to avoid clumping when stir-frying. Set aside.

Wash carrots, red bell pepper, onion, spring onions, celery and garlic with water. Cut into small pieces and then save for later use.

Prepare a wok with 3 tablespoons of vegetable oil. Turn on stove to medium flame. When oil is hot and shimmering, sauté garlic and onion until garlic turns brown and onion is translucent. Now, add carrots, celery and red bell pepper. Pour 1 tablespoon of light soy sauce and stir-fry for 2-3 minutes. Add 4 cups of cooked rice and turn stove to high flame. Stir continuously for about 5 minutes. Season with salt, black pepper and chili powder. Mix all ingredients well and stir-fry for another 5 minutes. Sprinkle with chopped spring onions and serve hot to 5-6 persons.

Health Tips:

- Eating celery can bring many benefits in your body. It contains potassium that is good for the kidneys and the heart. It also has many minerals that can help treat rheumatism, arthritis, migraines, and even asthma.

Vietnamese Watermelon Jelly

Ingredients:

- 1 big watermelon
- 4 tablespoon sugar
- 1 teaspoon maple syrup
- 1 pack jelly powder
- food coloring (preferably watermelon color)
- 1 cup water

Utensils Needed:

- Pot
- Ladle
- Large mixing bowl
- Wooden spatula for mixing
- Kitchen knife
- Chopping board
- Strainer

Directions:

Prepare 1 large watermelon. Make sure the outer layer is intact; this will ensure that the gelatin mixture won't leak when doing watermelon jelly. Wash watermelon with water and cut into half. Scrape off the watermelon fruit leaving the hard outer layer skin. Save this 2 half pieces of watermelon for later use.

Remove the seeds from the watermelon flesh fruit. Squeeze out watermelon fresh to get the watermelon water. Set aside the watermelon water.

In a large mixing bowl, combine 4 tablespoons of sugar, 1 pack jelly powder, a drop of food coloring and a teaspoon of maple syrup. Mix well.

In a pot, pour 1 cup of water and boil. Slowly add

the gelatin mixture and stir until gelatin melts. Turn off your stove and quickly add watermelon water into the pot. Stir thoroughly. Transfer the mixture into the 2 half pieces of watermelon and then refrigerate for a couple of hours. Cut into triangular pieces and serve chilled to 7-8 persons.

Health Tips:

- Watermelon is mostly made of water. It's good during summer because it relieves dehydration and cools the body. If you're in a beach or just experiencing hot weather, watermelon is the best fruit for you.

Tofu in Tomato Sauce

Ingredients:

- 500 grams tofu (cubed)
- 300 grams tomatoes (diced)
- 2 tablespoon light soy sauce
- 3 tablespoon vegetable oil
- 1 teaspoon black pepper
- 2 tablespoon spring onions (chopped)
- ½ teaspoon chili powder
- 2 cloves garlic (chopped)

Utensils Needed:

- Wok
- Spatula
- Cleaver
- Chopping board
- Mixing bowl
- Small wooden spatula

Directions:

Wash and drain 500 grams of tofu. Press to remove excess fluids. Rinse tomatoes, garlic, and spring onions and then chop. Save for later use.

In a mixing bowl, make your tomato sauce by combining 2 tablespoons of light soy sauce, 1-teaspoon black pepper, chopped garlic, ½-teaspoon chili powder and 300 grams of diced tomatoes. Pound or smash the tomatoes to extract juice while mixing. Set aside.

Prepare a wok or frying pan. Turn your stove on medium flame. Add 3 tablespoons of vegetable oil in the wok. Stir-fry tofu until golden on both sides. Pour tomato sauce into the wok and mix well with the fried tofu. Let it simmer for 3-4 minutes and then sprinkle 2 tablespoons of chopped spring onions. Good for 4-5 persons. Best serve with rice.

Health Tips:

- Tomatoes are rich in Lycopene. It helps reduce the risk of many cardiovascular diseases. Eating tomatoes can make your heart healthier by reducing bad cholesterol level in the body. This means formation of fats in the major blood vessels of the heart is reduced by eating tomatoes.

Water Spinach with Garlic Sauce

Ingredients:

- 500 grams water spinach (cut into 3 inches long)
- 6 cloves garlic (minced)
- 2 tablespoon light soy sauce
- 1 teaspoon black pepper
- 2 tablespoon olive oil
- ¼ cup vegetable stock
- 2 teaspoon cornstarch

Utensils Needed:

- Frying pan or skillet
- Spatula
- Kitchen knife
- Chopping board

Directions:

Wash water spinach with cold water. Cut off the lower end of the stalk and then cut into 3 inches long. Discard any dried or yellowish leaves. Rinse 5 cloves of garlic with water and remove the husk. Mince and set aside.

Heat 2 tablespoons of olive oil in a frying pan. Add garlic and sauté until golden. Pour 2 tablespoons of light soy sauce, ¼ cup of vegetable stock into the frying pan. Add 500 grams of chopped water spinach and stir until sauce coats the spinach completely. Cover the frying pan and let it simmer for 5-7 minutes. Stir occasionally and cook until water spinach is tender. Serve warm with rice to 5-6 persons.

Health Tips:

- Garlic acts as an antibacterial agent. It has always been used in the past to treat wounds and until now, many are still using garlic as a natural remedy to heal cuts or wounds. Garlic can also decrease bacteria formation inside your mouth.

Vietnamese Sesame Balls (Banh Ran or Banh Cam)

Ingredients:

- 150 grams mung beans (washed and soaked)
- 3 tablespoon agave syrup
- 1 tablespoon olive oil
- 100 grams coconut (shredded)
- 300 grams sticky rice flour
- 3 tablespoon all-purpose flour
- 2 tablespoon potato flakes
- 250 ml warm water
- 1/2 tsp salt
- 4 tablespoon white sugar
- 120 grams sesame seeds
- 3-4 cups Vegetable oil (for deep fry)

Utensils Needed:

- Large Skillet
- Strainer
- Large Mixing bowl
- Kitchen disposable gloves
- Plastic wrap
- Baking pan
- Rice cooker
- Blender
- Hand mixer

Directions:

Prepare ingredients for sesame balls fillings. Cook mung beans in a rice cooker until soft. Then transfer to a blender. Add shredded coconut, agave syrup and olive oil. Pulse until smooth. Save for later use.

In a large mixing bowl, combine all ingredients for making the sesame balls dough. Put sticky rice flour, all-purpose flour, lukewarm water, sugar and potato flakes into the bowl. Sprinkle with salt. Get a hand mixer and whisk the dough until even. Wear kitchen disposable gloves and knead well. Cover the large bowl with a plastic wrap and let it stand for about an hour. After an hour, place the dough in a baking pan and divide equally into small balls. Flatten each ball and put the mung beans filling at the center of each ball. Bring each corner of the flattened balls at the center to cover the mung beans filling. Shape the dough to form balls and roll on a plate with sesame seeds.

Prepare a large skillet with 3-4 cups of vegetable oil. Deep-fry the sesame balls until golden. Drain excess oil and place on a plate with paper towel. Serve hot to 4-5 persons.

Health Tips:

- Do you want your hair to look healthy and smooth? Mung beans contain copper, which is an important mineral that helps improve hair strength and growth. Making recipes out of mung beans will definitely keep your hair stronger and look better.

Vietnamese Rice Porridge

Ingredients:

- ½ cup sticky or glutinous rice
- 7 cups water
- 7 cups vegetable stock
- 2 cups plain rice
- 3 tablespoons vegan fish sauce or light soy sauce
- 2 teaspoon sugar
- 1 teaspoon black pepper
- 1 tablespoon cilantro (chopped)
- 2 tablespoon spring onions (chopped)

Utensils Needed:

- Pot
- Ladle
- Kitchen knife
- Chopping board

Directions:

Wash plain rice and glutinous rice with water. Wash at least 3-4 times. Prepare other ingredients like light soy sauce or vegan fish sauce. Chop cilantro and spring onions for garnishing the porridge after cooking.

Place in a pot of water with vegetable stock. Turn your stove on medium flame and cook the porridge. Stir frequently while cooking. Add vegan fish sauce or light soy sauce, sugar, and black pepper into the pot. Then mix all ingredients well using a ladle. Cover the pot and let it simmer for 15 minutes over low heat. Sprinkle with chopped onions and cilantro and serve hot to 6-7 persons.

Health Tips:

- Spring onion is good for your digestive system due to its fiber content. Eating spring onions will prevent you from having any gastrointestinal problems like stomachache or indigestion.

Vietnamese Mung Beans Sweet Dessert

Ingredients:

- 1 cup mung beans
- 2 cup coconut milk
- 4 cups water
- 1/2 cup cane sugar
- ½ cup coconut cream

Utensils Needed:

- Pot
- Ladle

Directions:

Rinse and soak mung beans with water for a couple of hours. Remove any floating mung beans.

In a pot, pour 4 cups of water and bring to a boil over medium heat. Add ½ cup of cane sugar and vigorously stir to dissolve the sugar in the water. Add 1-cup mung beans and mix. Cover the pot and lower the heat. Let it simmer until mung beans are soft. Now, add ½ cup of coconut cream and 2 cups of coconut milk. Whisk all ingredients and turn off your stove. Let it cool at a room temperature for 15 minutes and then place it in the refrigerator for at 30 minutes to an hour. Serve chilled to 5-6 persons.

Health Tips:

- Coconut milk is a good vegan alternative for dairy milk. It contains Selenium, which acts as an anti-oxidant that can relieve joint inflammation like arthritis. If you are suffering from any joint problem, you should consider using coconut milk in your recipes.

Carrot and Daikon Pickles Vietnamese Style

Ingredients:

- 1 large daikon (julienned)
- 1 large carrot (julienned)
- 3/4 cup water
- 1/2 cup rice vinegar
- 1 tablespoon salt

Utensils Needed:

- Large mixing bowl
- Small wooden spatula or spoon
- Covered Jar
- Mandoline
- Disposable kitchen gloves

Directions:

Wash carrot and daikon with water and then peel. Cut into thin strips by using a mandoline. Set aside.

Get a large mixing bowl and combine all your pickle ingredients. Start by adding sugar and rice vinegar first and then followed by salt. Stir the mixture with a wooden spoon. Now, add strips of carrots and daikon into the bowl. Toss all ingredients manually by hand. Make sure to wear disposable kitchen gloves when missing the ingredients. Pour ¾ cups of water and then place in a jar to store for at least 1 week. You can also serve this right away as a side dish. Good for 5-6 persons.

Health Tips:

- Are you having a stuffed nose? Then you should be

adding Daikon in your meal. Daikon is a good natural remedy for colds. You can simply mix it with ginger to get the best effect.

Hot and Spicy Tofu with Lemongrass Sauce

Ingredients:

- 500 grams tofu (cubed)
- 2 lemongrass stalks (minced)
- 2 cloves garlic (minced)
- 1 medium size onion (minced)
- 3 tablespoon vegetable oil
- 5-6 Thai bird chilies (minced)
- 1 tablespoon tamari sauce
- 1 teaspoon turmeric
- 2 teaspoon sugar
- 1 teaspoon salt
- 1 tablespoon chopped basil leaves

Utensils Needed:

- Frying pan
- Spatula
- Cleaver
- Chopping board
- Mixing bowl
- Wooden spatula or spoon (for mixing)

Directions:

Prepare all your ingredients and wash with water. Drain and press 500 grams of tofu and then cut into cubes. Cut vegetables into small pieces and then set aside.

Get a mixing bowl and combine minced lemongrass, tamari sauce, minced chili, turmeric, sugar, salt, and onion. Mix well and then soak the cubed tofu into the bowl for at least an hour. Save for later use.

In a frying pan, add 3 tablespoons of vegetable oil. Sauté garlic until golden and then add the tofu mixture into the frying pan. Stir-fry for until tofu is slightly crisp. Lower the heat and let it simmer until sauce is reduced. Now, add basil leaves and stir-fry for another minute. Serve warm with rice to 5 persons.

Health Tips:
- Turmeric powder has a main component called Curcumin, which can enhance the happy hormones in your brain. This means you will feel happier and more relaxed. If you're having a bad day, make sure to cook a dish with a pinch of turmeric and your sadness will go away.

Tofu with Broccoli in Sweet and Spicy Almond Sauce

Ingredients:

- 500 grams tofu (diced)
- 500 grams broccoli (cut into florets)
- 3 cloves garlic (minced)
- 2 inches ginger (minced)
- 1 large onion (chopped)
- 1 tablespoon sugar
- 5 pcs red chili (minced)
- ¼ cup almond butter
- ¼ cup warm water
- 1 tablespoon light soy sauce
- 1 tablespoon rice vinegar
- 1 teaspoon salt

Utensils Needed:

- Mixing bowl
- Wooden Spoon
- Wok
- Spatula
- Kitchen knife
- Chopping board

Directions:

Rinse and drain tofu and then dice. Wash broccoli with water and cut into florets. Save for later use.

In a mixing bowl, combine almond butter and warm water first. Make sure the mixture is smooth before adding all the other ingredients. Add light soy sauce, sugar, minced chili, and vinegar into the bowl. Set aside.

Prepare a wok. Heat 3 tablespoons of vegetable oil. Sauté garlic, onion and ginger. When onion turns translucent, add tofu and stir-fry until slightly brown. Now, add the broccoli florets and stir-fry until slightly tender. Pour the almond sauce mixture into the wok and mix all ingredients thoroughly. Cover the wok and let it simmer for 5-7 minutes. When the sauce thickens, it's ready to be served. Good for 5-7 persons, and best eaten with rice.

Health Tips:
- Broccoli is one of the best anti-cancer vegetables. It contains Glucoraphanin; a compound that transforms into Sulforaphane inside the body. Sulforaphane acts as a potent anti-cancer compound that helps the body to get rid of free radical damage, and as well as to remove bacteria and viruses out of the body.

Scallion Cake Vietnamese Style

Ingredients:

- 400 grams scallions (minced)
- 1 cup all-purpose flour
- 1 cup boiling water
- 3 tablespoon peanut oil
- 1 teaspoon olive oil
- 2 teaspoon salt

Utensils Needed:

- Frying pan
- Spatula
- Baking sheet
- Rolling pin
- Kitchen knife
- Chopping board

Directions:

Prepare 400 grams of scallion. Rinse with water and mince. Transfer to a bowl and combine with 2 teaspoons of salt. Set aside.

Get another mixing bowl and put 1 cup of all-purpose flour into the bowl. Add 1 cup of boiling water and mix using a metal beater. When the dough is warm, knead it manually by hands. Wear disposable kitchen gloves when kneading. Once the dough turns smooth, shape it into a ball and put in the bowl. Cover the bowl and let it stand for an hour.

Prepare a baking sheet and rolling pin. Spread some olive oil on the baking sheet and rolling pin to prevent the dough from sticking when preparing the scallion pancake. Get the prepared dough and divide it equally into 5 pieces. Form each piece into a ball and flatten using a rolling pin. Spread the prepared scallion and salt mixture at the center of each dough. Roll the dough and form again into a ball. Compress the dough using a rolling pin and save for frying.

In a frying pan, heat 3 tablespoons of peanut oil. Once the oil is hot, fry the scallion pancake until golden on both sides. Transfer to a plate with paper towel to remove excess oil. Serve hot to 5 persons.

Health Tips:

- Scallions help lower bad cholesterol level in the body and this means preventing you from having any serious cardiovascular problem like a heart attack.

Vietnamese Vegan Spring Rolls

Ingredients:
- 12 pieces fresh lettuce leaves
- 12 pieces rice paper
- 2 cups vermicelli noodles (cooked
- 2 cups fresh bean sprouts
- ½ cup mint leaves
- 1 cup carrots (julienned)
- 2 teaspoon salt
- 1 tablespoon apple cider vinegar
- 2 tablespoon light soy sauce
- 3 tablespoon water
- 1 tablespoon sugar
- 3 tablespoon peanut butter
- 2 teaspoon chili paste

Utensils Needed:
- Baking sheet or baking pan
- Kitchen Knife
- Chopping board
- Mixing bowl
- Wooden spoon
- Pot
- Colander

Directions:

Prepare all your vegetables and cut into the desired shape. Save for later use.

Cook noodles in a pot of boiling water for 4-5 minutes. Drain and rinse with cold water. Cut into 3 equal parts. Set aside.

Get a mixing bowl. Combine bean sprouts, carrots, mint leaves and cooked noodles into the bowl. Add salt and mix well.

Prepare your rice paper. Soak in water and then place

on a baking sheet or baking pan. Put lettuce on the corner of the rice paper. Then, place the mixed noodles and vegetables on the lettuce. Roll and secure the rice paper. Do the same procedure with all the vegetables and rice paper.

Now, prepare your sauce. Get a small mixing bowl. Add peanut butter, light soy sauce, vinegar, sugar, and chili paste. Stir to combine all the ingredients. Serve the spring rolls with sauce to 10-12 persons.

Health Tips:

- Lettuce is packed with Vitamin A. When you eat food high in Vitamin A, your skin and vision is enhanced. Getting enough Vitamin A can also prevent you from having serious skin and eye problem when you get older.
- Mint leaves can help in treating nausea and vomiting. This is especially beneficial to pregnant women during their 1st trimester, when morning sickness happens.

Caramelized Tofu Vietnamese Style

Ingredients:

- 400 grams tofu (cut into cubes)
- 4 tablespoon white cane sugar
- 2 garlic cloves (minced)
- 1 medium onion (minced)
- 1 tablespoon light soy sauce
- 2 tablespoon olive oil
- 1 teaspoon salt
- 2 tablespoon water
- 2 tablespoon green onions (chopped)

Utensils Needed:

- Skillet
- Spatula
- Chopping board
- Cleaver

Directions:

Rinse tofu with water and then drain excess fluids by pressing. Chop green onions and save for garnish later.

In a skillet, heat 2 tablespoons of olive oil and sauté garlic and onion. Add cubed tofu and stir-fry until slightly brown on both sides. Now, add water, light soy sauce, salt and sugar. Mix thoroughly over low heat. When sugar melts, turn off your stove and continue mixing all the ingredients. Transfer to a plate and garnish with chopped green onions. Good for 4 persons.

Health Tips:

- Cane sugar is good for Type 1 Diabetes because it has

a low glycemic index. This means, blood sugar level is maintained and won't spike up when eating food with cane sugar. For people with Type 2 Diabetes, eating food with cane sugar should be in control.

Vietnamese Vegan Banh Mi

Ingredients:

- 1 piece vegan baguette (28 inches long)
- 1 medium cucumber (cut thinly)
- 1 carrot (julienned)
- 1 daikon (julienned)
- 1 teaspoon salt
- 2 teaspoon light soy sauce
- 1 tablespoon vegan mayonnaise
- 1 teaspoon chili sauce
- 1 jalapeno pepper (cut thinly)
- 1 tablespoon cilantro
- 7 tablespoon rice vinegar
- 2 teaspoon sugar

Utensils Needed:

- Mixing bowl
- Wooden spoon or spatula
- Bread knife
- Oven

Directions:

Rinse all vegetables with water and pat to dry. Remove peeling and cut into thin strips. Save for later use.

In a mixing bowl, combine vinegar, light soy sauce, vegan mayonnaise, sugar, chili sauce, and salt. Mix well. Now, add the julienned vegetables. Let it stand for an hour.

Cut vegan Baguette into 4 quarters. Spread the vegetable mixture on the baguette. Preheat oven to 370-degree Celsius. Bake for 3 minutes only, just enough to make the bread crispy. Serve warm to 4 persons.

Health Tips:

- Jalapeno is rich in Vitamin C. This vitamin is important to keep your immune system strong. When your immune system is strong, you keep yourself away from many illnesses.

Longan and Lotus Seed Sweet Soup

Ingredients:

- 250 grams lotus seeds
- 150 grams longan
- 4 cups water
- 1 teaspoon baking soda
- 1 teaspoon vanilla extract
- 6 tablespoons sugar
- 1 tablespoon agave nectar

Utensils Needed:

- Pot
- Colander
- Saucepan
- Ladle
- Kitchen knife
- Chopping board
- Mixing bowl
- Wooden spatula

Directions:

Rinse and drain lotus seeds. Soak lotus seed in warm water for a couple of hours or overnight. Cook in a pot of boiling water over low flame. Add 1 teaspoon of baking soda and let it simmer for an hour or 2 hours until lotus seeds become soft. Drain and remove the outer green layer. Crush slightly and set aside.

In a saucepan, add 4 cups of water. Boil and add Longan and lotus seeds. Pour agave nectar and add sugar into the saucepan. Add 2 teaspoons of vanilla extract and stir well. Cover the saucepan and bring to a simmer. Cook for 30 minutes. Stir occasionally while cooking. Serve warm to 4-5 persons.

Health Tips:
- Lotus seed is a natural sedative. If you're having a hard time to sleep at night, prepare a meal made of lotus seed and you will surely feel relaxed and calm.

Vietnamese Vegan Crepes

Ingredients:

- 250 grams rice flour
- 1 can coconut milk
- 1 cup water
- 1 teaspoon turmeric powder
- 1 teaspoon salt
- 2 scallions (minced)
- Vegetable oil for frying
- 100 grams asparagus (trimmed and cut into 3 inches long)
- 100 grams mushrooms (chopped)
- 2 large white onion (sliced)
- 2 large tomatoes (chopped)
- 2 tablespoon mint leaves (chopped)
- 100 grams bean sprouts
- 200 grams lettuce
- 2 tablespoon coriander leaves (chopped)
- 2 tablespoon light soy sauce
- 2 tablespoon lime juice
- 2 tablespoon rice vinegar
- 2 teaspoon pepper
- 2 tablespoon sugar

Utensils Needed:

- Frying Pan
- Spatula
- Kitchen Knife
- Chopping board
- Baking sheet
- Mixing bowl
- Non-stick pan
- Hand mixer
- Wooden spoon

Directions:

Prepare all the vegetables and cut into your desired shape. In a frying pan, heat vegetable oil and sauté onions until translucent. Add mushrooms, asparagus, and bean sprouts. Cook until slightly tender. Drain excess oil and save for later use.

Get a mixing bowl and combine sauce mixture. Add light soy sauce, vinegar, lime juice, salt, pepper, and sugar. Whisk until sugar dissolves completely. Set aside.

In a large mixing bowl, put rice flour, water, coconut milk, scallion, salt and turmeric powder. Use a hand mixer to combine all ingredients well. Cover the bowl with a plastic wrap and let it stand for an hour.

In a non-stick frying pan, put vegetable oil. Tilt the pan to spread the oil. Pour crepe mixture just enough to cover the pan. Fry both sides of the crepe until golden. You will know that the crepe is ready for flipping on its other side when bubbles are starting to form on the surface. Transfer crepe on a baking sheet and place lettuce, tomatoes, mint leaves, and coriander on the crepe. Add sautéed mushroom, asparagus, onions and bean sprouts. Pour some sauce mixture evenly on top of the vegetables. Fold the crepe and serve warm to 4-5 persons.

Health Tips:
- Asparagus is a natural diuretic. It helps remove toxins out of your body. Eating asparagus will prevent you from urinary tract infections.
- Coriander is a common herb in Vietnam and is usually used in most dishes. It promotes good digestion and prevents you from having stomach problems like indigestion, stomach cramps, and constipation. It contains rich amount of fiber and enzymes that are beneficial to your gastrointestinal system.

Vietnamese Mixed Vegetable Salad

Ingredients:

- 1 cabbage (shredded)
- 1 carrot (julienned)
- ½ cup bean sprouts
- 250 grams rice noodles (cooked)
- 150 grams tofu (cubed)
- 3 tablespoons lemon juice
- 2 tablespoons light soy sauce
- 1 teaspoon salt
- 2-3 pcs red chili (minced)
- 1 garlic clove (minced)
- 1 tablespoon vegetable oil (for frying)
- 1 tablespoon cilantro leaves (chopped)

Utensils Needed:

- Mixing Bowl
- Wooden spatula
- Kitchen knife
- Mandoline
- Chopping board
- Frying pan
- Spatula

Directions:

Wash vegetables and cut into thin strips. Rinse and drain tofu and cut into cubes.

Cook rice noodles in a pot of boiling water for 3-5 minutes. Drain and place on a plate. Save for later use.

In a frying pan, heat 1 tablespoon of vegetable oil. Stir-fry tofu until slightly brown. Add cabbage, carrot and bean sprouts. Cook for 2 minutes while continuously stirring. Transfer to a plate with paper towel to remove excess oil.

In a mixing bowl, combine light soy sauce, lemon juice, salt, garlic, and minced chili. Mix well. Add tofu and vegetables into the bowl and toss thoroughly.

Put salad on top of the cooked rice noodles and mix. Good for 4 persons.

Health Tips:

- Bean sprouts can improve your brain cognitive function as well as your nerves. It contains a lot of Vitamin B like Vitamin B6, B12 and folic acid. If you want to avoid diseases like Alzheimer's disease and Parkinson's, you must eat food rich in Vitamin B.

Tofu Noodle Soup with Broccoli and Bean Sprouts

Ingredients:

- 250 grams rice noodles
- 1 broccoli head (cut into florets)
- 150 grams mushrooms (chopped)
- 150 grams tofu (diced)
- 1 large onion (minced)
- 3 tablespoons light soy sauce
- 1 tablespoon brown rice vinegar
- 1 teaspoon mint
- 1 teaspoon salt
- 1 teaspoon garlic powder
- 1 teaspoon ginger powder
- 1 teaspoon sesame oil
- 3 – 4 cups water
- 1 teaspoon pepper
- ½ teaspoon chili powder

Utensils Needed:

- Strainer or colander
- Pot
- Ladle
- Kitchen knife
- Chopping board

Directions:

Cook rice noodles in a pot of boiling water. Cook just until noodle is al dente. Drain and save for later use.

In a pot over medium heat. Add 1 tablespoon of sesame oil. Sauté onion until translucent. Now, pour 3-4 cups of water into the pot and add chopped broccoli and mushrooms. Cook until tender and then add diced tofu. Add seasonings; light soy sauce, vinegar, mint, chili powder, garlic powder, salt, pepper, and ginger powder. Mix all ingredients with a ladle. Cover the pot and let it simmer for 7-10 minutes. Add cooked noodles and serve right away. Good for 6 persons.

Health Tips:

- The brown rice vinegar is a good antiseptic remedy for wounds and cut. It has always been used as a traditional herbal treatment for wound infections in the past and until now.

Red Bean Sweet Soup Vietnamese Style

Ingredients:

- 300 grams red beans
- 50 grams tapioca pearls
- 1 cup coconut milk
- ¼ cup coconut cream
- ½ cup sugar
- 1 teaspoon agave nectar
- 2 teaspoon tapioca starch
- 1 cup water
- 1 teaspoon salt

Utensils Needed:

- Pot
- Strainer
- Ladle
- Kitchen knife
- Chopping board
- Strainer

Directions:

Prepare tapioca pearls. Cook in a pot of boiling water until it turns transparent. Drain and set aside.

In a saucepan, heat coconut milk and coconut cream. Add sugar and agave nectar. Mix well and simmer for 5 minutes. Let it cool and save for later use.

In a pot, add 1 cup of water. Put red beans and cook until soft. Add salt and stir occasionally. Now, put the cooked tapioca pearls and add 2 teaspoons of tapioca starch. Simmer for 5 minutes until soup thickens. Transfer into small bowls. Pour coconut milk mixture into each bowl. Serve warm or chilled to 4 persons.

Health Tips:

- Red beans or Adzuki beans contain protein that controls blood sugar level in the body. The protein found in red beans prevents the breaking down of complex carbohydrates that can result in an increased blood sugar.

Vietnamese Pomelo Sweet Soup

Ingredients:

- 1 large pomelo fruit (cut into small pieces)
- 200 grams mung beans
- ¾ cups sugar
- 2 teaspoon salt
- 5 grams alum
- 1 cup coconut milk
- 1 teaspoon corn starch
- ½ cup coconut cream
- 1 cup tapioca starch
- ½ cup of water

Utensils Needed:

- Pot
- saucepan
- Ladle
- Kitchen knife
- Chopping board
- Colander

Directions:

Wash and prepare 1 large pomelo fruit. Remove the hard outer layer and leave the white soft layer inside. Cut the white pomelo layer into strips and then slice into small bite pieces. Set aside. Take out the pomelo fruit flesh and squeeze out the juice. Save this for cooking later.

Soak mung beans in a bowl of water for a couple of hours. Cook in a pot of water until soft. Drain the mung beans and discard the water. Let it cool and save for later use.

Prepare a saucepan. Heat coconut milk and coconut cream. Add ¾-cup sugar, and cornstarch. Mix until sugar dissolves. Set aside.

Boil the pomelo white layer pieces in a pot of water. Add alum and salt. Cook until soft. Drain the pomelo and soak in tapioca starch. Make sure to cover the pomelo white layer meat with starch. Set aside.

Get your prepared coconut milk mixture. Combine mung beans, pomelo white layer meat with tapioca starch, and pomelo extract. Add ½ cup of water and stir all ingredients. Cover the saucepan and bring it to a simmer. Cook for 5-7 minutes while constantly stirring.

Health Tips:
- Pomelo is a great fruit for keeping your body slim. It contains an enzyme called Carnitine palmitoyl-transferase. This enzyme speeds up metabolism and burns fat in the body. If you're health and body conscious, start eating pomelo right after your workouts.

Cucumber Salad Vietnamese Style

Ingredients:

- 1 cucumber (sliced)
- 2 tablespoons rice vinegar
- 1 tablespoon lime juice
- 1 tablespoon lime zest
- 1 tablespoon vegan fish sauce
- 1 teaspoon salt
- 2 teaspoon sugar
- 2 garlic cloves (minced)
- 1 teaspoon chili paste
- ½ teaspoon black pepper

Utensils Needed:

- Mixing bowl
- Mortar and Pestle
- Wooden spatula
- Cleaver
- Chopping board

Directions:

Wash cucumber with water and remove the skin. Cut into slices and transfer to a mixing bowl.

Pound peanuts with mortar and pestle and then save for garnish later.

Get your bowl of sliced cucumbers. Add vegan fish sauce, rice vinegar, lime juice, and sugar. Mix all ingredients. Add lime zest, salt, pepper and chili paste. Toss with a wooden spoon and make sure to coat the cucumbers well with the salad dressing.

Garnish with crushed peanuts and serve right away. You can also put it in the refrigerator and serve chilled. Good for 4 persons.

Health Tips:

- Cucumbers are commonly prepared as a salad in Vietnam. It is also good for the brain. It contains Fisetin, a compound that improves memory and cognitive function.

Chayote Stir-Fry Recipe

Ingredients:

- 1 large Chayote (chopped)
- 1 large onion (chopped)
- 3 cloves garlic (minced)
- 1 tablespoon vegan fish sauce
- 1 teaspoon sugar
- ½ teaspoon pepper
- 1 teaspoon salt
- 1 tablespoon vegetable oil

Utensils Needed:

- Frying pan
- Spatula
- Chopping board
- Kitchen knife

Directions:

Wash Chayote with water and then remove the skin. Cut into small bite pieces and set aside. Rinse onion and garlic with water and then mince. Save for sautéing later.

In a frying pan, add 1 tablespoon of vegetable oil. Sauté garlic and onion when the oil is hot and shimmering. Stir-fry chopped chayote until tender. Season with sugar, salt and pepper. Add 1 tablespoon of vegan fish sauce and mix all ingredients well.

Serve with hot rice. Good for 4 persons.

Health Tips:

- If you're planning to have a baby, make sure to cook dishes with Chayote. Chayote contains a good amount of Folate. Pregnant women needs ample amounts of Folate because it reduces the risk of having birth defects for the unborn child.

Banana with Coconut Milk Vietnamese Dessert

Ingredients:

- 500 grams ripe bananas (sliced)
- 1 cup coconut milk
- ½ cup coconut cream
- ½ cup sugar
- 4 tablespoons tapioca pearls
- ½ teaspoon salt
- 1 tablespoon sesame seeds
- 2 tablespoons peanuts (crushed)
- 1 teaspoon Pandan extract
- 1 cup water
-

Utensils Needed:

- Pot
- Ladle
- Kitchen knife
- Chopping board

Directions:

Peel the banana skin and cut into small bite pieces. Set aside.

Cook your tapioca pearls in a pot of boiling water for about 5 minutes or until it turns transparent. Then. Let it cool at a room temperature.

Now, heat a saucepan and add 1 cup of water. Put Pandan extract and simmer for 2 minutes. Add coconut milk, coconut cream, sugar, salt and cooked tapioca pearls. Stir and combine all ingredients. Cover the saucepan and let it simmer for 5 minutes. Stir occasionally while cooking. Reduce the heat and add sliced bananas. Cook for another 1-2 minutes. Serve hot or chilled with crushed peanuts and sesame seeds on top. Good for 3 persons.

Health Tips:
- Bananas are good for diabetics. It tastes sweet and you will think that it's not good for diabetic people, but bananas contain pectin and resistant starch that helps maintain a normal blood sugar level. Eating bananas can make you feel full and it also delays stomach emptying. This way, your blood sugar level won't spike up after eating meals.

Vietnamese Spinach Soup with Tofu

Ingredients:

- 500 grams Vietnamese Malabar Spinach (chopped)
- 400 grams tofu (diced)
- 1 tablespoon cane sugar
- 2 cups vegetable stock
- 3 cups water
- 1 teaspoon salt
- ½ teaspoon pepper

Utensils Needed:

- Pot
- Ladle
- Kitchen Knife
- Chopping board

Directions:

Wash Malabar spinach thoroughly. Remove any dried or yellowish leaves. Chop into 3 equal parts. Set aside. Rinse and drain 400 grams of tofu. Cut into small cubes and save for later use.

In a pot, pour 2 cups of vegetable stock and 3 cups of water. Heat the pot over medium flame. Add Malabar spinach and cubed tofu. Cover the pot and bring to a boil. Then, add salt, sugar and pepper. Mix all ingredients with a ladle. Cover the pot again and simmer for 2-3 minutes. Serve hot to 4-5 persons.

Health Tips:

- Malabar spinach is a good source of Vitamin A, beta-carotene and lutein. These are all beneficial for your eyes. Eating Malabar spinach can improve your vision as well as prevent you from acquiring eye diseases as you get older.

Stir-Fried Chayote with Broccoli

Ingredients:

- 2 medium size Chayote (sliced)
- 1 head Broccoli (cut into small florets)
- 1 tablespoon vegetable oil
- ¼ cup vegetable broth
- 1 inch ginger (minced)
- 1 garlic clove (minced)
- 1 teaspoon salt
- ½ teaspoon black pepper
- 2 teaspoons spearmint leaves (chopped)

Utensils Needed:

- Skillet
- Spatula
- Cleaver
- Chopping board

Directions:

Wash broccoli and chayote with water. Remove the skin of chayote and cut into small bite sizes. Cut broccoli into small florets and set aside. Mince ginger and garlic for stir-frying later.

Prepare a skillet. Heat 1 tablespoon of vegetable oil. Sauté garlic and ginger when the oil is already hot. Stir-fry chayote first for at least 2-3 minutes or just until tender. Add broccoli and stir-fry for another 2-3 minutes. Pour ¼ cup of vegetable broth into the skillet and season with salt and black pepper. Cover the skillet and let it simmer for 2 minutes. Serve warm with spearmint on top. Good for 4-5 persons.

Health Tips:

- Vietnamese cooking commonly used different herbs for cooking. One of this herb is spearmint. Spearmint is a herbal plant that maintains a normal hormone balance in your body. It directly acts with your endocrine system and stimulates it to keep your hormones in balance.

Vietnamese Kohlrabi Salad

Ingredients:

- 1 large kohlrabi (julienned)
- 400 grams bean sprouts
- 1 medium carrot (julienned)
- 2 tablespoons coriander leaves (chopped)
- 3 shallots (julienned)
- 1 tablespoon light soy sauce
- 2 teaspoon lime juice
- 1 tablespoon olive oil
- 1 tablespoon rice wine vinegar
- 1 teaspoon salt
- 1 piece red chili (minced)
- 1 clove garlic (minced)
- 1 teaspoon sugar
- 1 tablespoon peanuts (crushed)
-

Utensils Needed:

- Mixing bowl
- Wooden Spatula
- Mandoline
- Kitchen knife
- Chopping board
- Mortar and pestle

Directions:

Wash all vegetables with cold running water. Peel the skin and cut into thin strips with a mandoline. Mince garlic and red chili with a cleaver and set aside. Pound peanuts with a mortar and pestle and save for later use.

In a mixing bowl, combine light soy sauce, vinegar, lime juice, salt, olive oil and sugar. Mix well. Now, add the s Kohlrabi, bean sprouts and carrots. Combine all ingredients thoroughly.

Add chopped coriander leaves and crushed peanuts before serving. Good for 4 persons. You may serve this right away or put it in a refrigerator for an hour, and then serve chilled.

Health Tips:
- Kohlrabi is a vegetable commonly used in Vietnam. It contains Iron and Calcium that both helps in the formation of red blood cells. Your body needs Calcium to be able to absorb Iron. Red blood cells are formed in the bones and Calcium keeps your bones strong.

Stir-Fried Bamboo Shoots with Tofu in Ginger Sauce

Ingredients:

- 500 grams tofu (cubed)
- 150 grams mixed mushrooms (cut into halves)
- 250 grams bamboo shoots (chopped)
- 2 cloves garlic (minced)
- 4 inches ginger (minced)
- ½ cup vegetable stock
- 2 tablespoons tamari sauce
- 1 tablespoon vegan fish sauce
- 1 teaspoon cornstarch
- 1 teaspoon sugar
- ½ teaspoon chili powder
- 2 tablespoons olive oil
- 1 tablespoon rice vinegar
- 1 tablespoon basil leaves (chopped)

Utensils Needed:

- Skillet
- Spatula
- Chopping board
- Cleaver

Directions:

Rinse and drain 500 grams of tofu. Press to remove excess fluids and cut into cubes. Wash 150 grams of mixed mushrooms, 250 grams of bamboo shoots, ginger and garlic. Mince ginger and garlic. Cut mushrooms into halves and slice the bamboo shoots into medium sizes.

In a skillet, heat 2 tablespoons of olive oil. Saute garlic until it turns brown. Add tofu, mushrooms, and bamboo shoots into the skillet. Stir-fry for 5-7 minutes until bamboo shoots are tender. Now, add ½ cup of vegetable stock and 1 teaspoon of cornstarch into the skillet. Mix until cornstarch dissolves completely. Add 2 tablespoons of tamari sauce, 1-tablespoon vegan fish sauce, 1-teaspoon sugar, ½-teaspoon chili powder and 1 tablespoon of rice vinegar. Toss all ingredients well. Cover the skillet and let it simmer for 3-5 minutes while stirring occasionally. Garnish with chopped basil leaves and serve warm to 5 persons.

Health Tips:

- Do you want to have a strong immune system to ward off diseases? Eating bamboo shoots can improve your immune system. It contains ample amounts of anti-oxidants and prevents you from having infections. A strong immune system is your first line of defense against invasion of bacteria and viruses.

Black Bean Sweet Vietnamese Dessert

Ingredients:

- 2 cups coconut milk
- ½ cup coconut cream
- 2 teaspoon salt
- 2 Pandan leaves
- 5 cups water
- ¾ cups sugar
- 1 tablespoon agave nectar
- 4 teaspoons tapioca flour
- 2 cups black beans
-

Utensils Needed:

- Pot
- Ladle
- Saucepan
- Small bowls

Directions:

Prepare a pot of boiling water. Add 2 cups of black beans, pandan leaves and 2-teaspoon salt. Cook over low flame for an hour and 30 minutes. Wait until black beans become soft before turning off your stove. Drain the beans and transfer into small bowls. Set aside.

Now, prepare a saucepan. Add coconut milk, coconut cream, sugar, agave nectar and tapioca flour into the saucepan. Cook for about 5 minutes while stirring continuously.

Pour the sweet coconut mixture into each bowl of black beans. Serve about 5 persons.

Health Tips:

- Iron is a vital mineral that your body needs. It aids

in the formation of red blood cells. Red blood cells carry oxygen throughout the body. This means Iron plays an important role in ensuring the transport of oxygen to all your body organs. Tapioca contains Iron and thus eating food with tapioca helps your body maintain a normal oxygen blood circulation.

Vietnamese Peanut Sticky Rice (Xoi Lac)

Ingredients:

- 1 cup sticky rice
- ½ cup peanuts (peeled)
- 1 teaspoon salt
- 1 teaspoon agave nectar
- 1 tablespoon vegetable oil
- 1 tablespoon sesame seeds

Utensils Needed:

- Pot
- Steamer
- Ladle
- Chopsticks

Directions:

Wash sticky rice with water for 3-4 times and then soak it in a bowl of water for a couple of hours.

Cook ½ cup of peanuts in a pot of boiling water. Add salt and then mix well. Let it cool at a room temperature after cooking.

Prepare a steamer. Place sticky rice on the steamer and add the cooked peanuts. Mix 1 teaspoon of agave nectar and combine all ingredients using a chopstick. Cook for about 15 minutes. Garnish with sesame seeds on top and serve warm to 4-5 persons.

Health Tips:

- Agave nectar contains Calcium. Adding agave in your dish will keep your bones and teeth strong, as well as it can help you maintain a normal blood pressure.

- Sesame seeds are good anti-bacterial and anti-inflammatory agents. It can help your wounds heal faster and prevent you from getting any infections.

Vietnamese Colorful Rice Cake

Ingredients:

- 4 cups rice flour
- 2 teaspoon active dry yeast (mixed with ½ cup warm water and 1 teaspoon sugar)
- ½ cup tapioca starch
- 2 ¼ cups water
- 1 ¾ cups sugar
- 4 teaspoon vanilla
- 2 cups coconut milk
- 1 cup water
- 1 tablespoon olive oil
- Vegan Food coloring (different colors)

Utensils Needed:

- Mixing bowls
- Hand mixer
- Steamer
- Molds
- Saucepan

Directions:

Get a mixing bowl, combine flour, tapioca starch and water. Mix until mixture is smooth. Add active dry yeast mixture into the bowl and stir thoroughly. Cover the bowl with a plastic wrap and let it stand for 2-3 hours.

In another mixing bowl, combine vanilla, sugar, coconut milk and water. Mix all ingredients well and pour into a saucepan. Heat the mixture over a high flame for 1-2 minutes. Turn off your stove and let it cool at a room temperature for 30 minutes.

Combine coconut milk mixture with flour mixture. Use a hand mixer to mix all the ingredients. Whisk until smooth. Add food coloring of your choice. You can also divide the mixture into different bowls to add different food colorings.

Spread olive oil into small molds. Transfer the rice cake mixture into the molds. Layer the molds in a steamer. Cook for about 5 minutes or until the rice cake starts to expand. Let the rice cakes cool at a room temperature before removing out of the molds. You can serve the rice cake warm or chilled.

Health Tips:

- Olive oil is mostly monounsaturated fats. It contains oleic acid that acts as an anti-inflammatory agent in the body. It also acts as an anti-oxidant, which is important to keep your cells healthy and prevent you from acquiring cancer-related diseases.

Sour Mushroom Soup Vietnamese Style

Ingredients:

- 350 grams mushrooms (cut into halves)
- 1 large tomato (chopped)
- 150 grams pineapple chunks
- 1 teaspoon salt
- 1 teaspoon black pepper
- 4 cups water
- 1 cup vegetable stock
- 2 tablespoon light soy sauce or vegan fish sauce
- 2 teaspoon sugar
- 1 large red onion (minced)
- 2 teaspoon cilantro leaves (minced)
- 2 teaspoon olive oil

Utensils Needed:

- Pot
- Ladle
- Kitchen knife
- Chopping board

Directions:

Prepare all your ingredients. Wash mushroom and cut off the stem. Slice mushroom caps into halves. Rinse onion, cilantro and tomato with water. Then, chop into small pieces.

In a pot, add 2 teaspoons of olive oil, just enough to sauté onion and tomato. Pour 4 cups of water and a cup of vegetable stock into the pot. Add light soy sauce, sugar, and pineapple chunks. Mix the ingredients and then cover the pot. Let it simmer for 5 minutes and then add the mushroom. Bring to a boil and cook for another 7 minutes. Sprinkle with salt and pepper. Stir occasionally while cooking. Serve hot to 5-6 persons

Health Tips:
- Red onion has a compound called Quercetin. This compound prevents cancer cells from increasing in the body and as well as inhibits tumor growth. Eating red onions can lower your risk of acquiring cancer diseases.

Vege-Thai-Rian

Ariya Netjoy Presents:

VEGANIZED

THAI RESTAURANT RECIPES

BE GOOD AND KIND TO ALL LIVING BEINGS
PRACTICE IT

Copyrights 2017 All rights reserved © Ariya Netjoy

No part of this publication or the information in it may be quoted from or reproduced in any form by means such as printing, scanning, photocopying, or otherwise without prior written permission of the copyright holder.

Sunny Thai Publishing

Terms of Use Disclaimer Efforts have been made to ensure that the information in this book is accurate. However, the author and the publisher do not hold any responsibility for errors, omissions, or contrary interpretation of the subject matter herein. The recipes provided in this book are for informational purposes only and are not intended to provide dietary advice. A medical practitioner should be consulted for dietary advice. Additionally, recipe cooking times may require adjustment depending on age and quality of appliances and tools. Readers are urged to take all needed precautions to ensure ingredients are fully cooked to avoid the dangers of foodborne illnesses. The author and publisher do not take any responsibility for any consequences that may result due to following the instructions provided in this book.

Thank you for being a loyal reader and friend. As a reward, we would like to bring even more delicious vegan and vegetarian dishes into your life, FREE! All you have to do, is sign up with your email and you are set. Everything is free and full of fun so come on and eat with us! Click the blue mail above. Available on the Kindle version.

Table of Contents

Introduction
Thai Coconut Mushroom Soup
Spicy Thai Green Mango Salad (Som Tum Mamuang)
Vegetarian Pad Thai
Chickpea Thai Curry
Stir-Fry Thai Mixed Vegetables with Garlic Peanut Sauce
Egg-free Thai Corn Fritters (Tod Man Khao Pod)
Vegetarian Thai Curry
Grilled Eggplant Thai-Style
Tofu with Curry Sauce
Coconut Thai Rice
Green Papaya Salad (Som Tam)
Vegetarian Thai Noodle Soup
Vegan Thai Steamed Dumplings with Spicy dipping sauce
Fried Tofu with Thai Peanut Sauce
Pomelo Thai Salad (Yum Som O)
Stir-Fried Thai Pumpkin Recipe
Thai Stir-fried Water Spinach (Pad Pak Boong)
Coconut Milk Pudding with Lime
Crunchy tofu with Thai Plum Sauce
Thai Stir-fried Broccoli florets
Fried Rice Thai-Style with Pineapple and Basil
Tofu with Asparagus and Kale in Peanut Curry Sauce
Vegan Thai Coconut Ice Cream
Carrot Salad Thai-Style
Tofu and mushroom with Green Curry Paste
Green Beans with Garlic Tamarind Sauce
Vegetarian Thai Spring Rolls with Sweet peanut sauce
Thai Rice Noodles with Tofu and Mushroom
Bananas in Coconut Milk

Asparagus with Spicy Curry Sauce
Celery Creamy Coconut Soup
Tofu Satay with Spicy Peanut Sauce
Cucumber Salad Thai-Style
Stir-Fry Mushroom and Basil Curry
Hot and Spicy Peanut Fried Rice
Mango Thai Pudding
Spicy Ginger Soup with Coconut Milk
Broccoli and Cauliflower Sweet Curry
Stir-Fry Sweet and Sour Potato Curry
Carrot Noodles with Tofu in Creamy Peanut Sauce
Thai Tomato Salad
Fried Chive Cake Thai-Style (Kanom Gui Chai)
Bitter Gourd with Garlic and Peanut Sauce
Stir-fried Sweet and Spicy Brussel Sprout
Sweet Taro Balls in Creamy Coconut Milk
Sautéed Bean Sprouts with Tofu
Thai Cassava Dessert with Coconut Milk
Orange Carrot Soup Thai-Style
Thai Sweet and Sour Tofu

Introduction

Thailand has the most flavorful vegetarian recipes worldwide. You can definitely indulge yourself in one single recipe and you get everything you need from spicy, sweet, salty, bitter and sour taste. It feels like magic, every recipe is delicious and unique.

Creativity and intricate cooking is common in Thai vegan dishes. Adding a lot of spices but keeping the ingredients well combined is distinctive to Thai recipes.

Thai cuisine is also known as one of the healthiest food in the world. Thai people are mostly Buddhist in nature and they follow certain rules like, not to kill, and live a healthy life by eating nutritious food. This is the main reason why Thai dishes includes a lot of medicinal herbs and spices. Therefore, if you want to stay fit and healthy, knowing that Thailand offers not just delectable recipes but healthy food, you should definitely try every vegan recipes found in Thailand restaurants.

In this cookbook, you can try many vegetarian recipes that are commonly found in food stalls and even fine dining restaurants in Thailand. This include vegetarian dishes that uses 3 important ingredients, these are coconut, curry and glutinous rice. From appetizers, main dishes to even desserts, these ingredients are most of the time present in every recipes. You will also get healthy tips in every recipe you learn from this cookbook. Enjoy cooking!

Thai Coconut Mushroom Soup

Ingredients:

- 1 can coconut milk (400ml)
- 2 cups mushroom (sliced)
- 4 cups vegetable broth
- 3 tablespoon light (thin) soy sauce
- 2 teaspoon vegetarian red curry paste
- 1 tablespoon lime juice
- 1 tablespoon lime zest
- 4 small garlic cloves (minced)
- 2 tablespoon ginger (grated)
- 1 bunch spring onions (finely chopped)
- 1 tablespoon coarsely chopped cilantro (garnish)
- 1 tablespoon vegetable oil
- 1 tablespoon brown sugar
- 1 stalk lemon grass (minced)
- Salt and pepper to taste

Utensils Needed:

- 2 Large pot or saucepan
- wok
- Coconut shell spoon (used as ladle for soup)
- Cleaver
- Chopping block
- Strainer
- Hand grater

Directions:

Prepare all the ingredients. Wash all the vegetables with clean cold water. Using a hand grater, grind the peeled ginger. Cut the mushroom caps with the use of a cleaver and a chopping block. Finely chop spring onions, lemongrass and garlic. Save for later use.

In a large pot, boil 4 cups of vegetable broth. Add 400ml

of coconut milk and bring to simmer over medium flame. Add the minced lemongrass and cook for 7-8 minutes. Using a strainer, discard the lemon grass and transfer the liquid mixture of coconut milk and vegetable broth to another pot.

In a wok, pour 1 tablespoon of vegetable oil and wait until hot before adding minced garlic and ginger. Add 2 cups pf sliced mushroom and sauté until slightly tender. Transfer the cooked mushrooms to the coconut milk pot and put the stove over medium heat. Add lime juice, lime zest, brown sugar, light soy sauce, red curry paste and the spring onions into the pot. Stir using a coconut shell spoon to mix all the ingredients well. Cover the pot and bring to simmer for about 6-7 minutes. Season with salt and pepper. Garnish with chopped cilantro. Serve hot to 4-5 persons.

Health Tips:
- Lemongrass has a substance called citral, which aids in good digestion. You won't suffer any stomachache or stomach spasm when you add lemongrass in your recipe.

Spicy Thai Green Mango Salad (Som Tum Mamuang)

Ingredients:

- 4 pieces green mangoes (peeled and shredded)
- 4 red Thai Chili (minced)
- 2 tablespoon olive oil
- 4 fresh string beans (cut into 1-2 inch long)
- 3 teaspoon coconut palm sugar
- 1 large clove garlic (peeled and minced)
- 4 tablespoon roasted peanuts (crushed)
- 3 tablespoon light soy sauce
- 3 tablespoon lime juice
- 2 small tomatoes (cut into halves)
- 3 shallots (cut into thin strips)
- Salt to taste
- Chopped cilantro (garnish)

Utensils Needed:

- Mortar and pestle (for grinding ingredients)
- Shredder (for cutting mangoes)
- Large mixing bowl
- Wooden spoon
- Cleaver
- Chopping block

Directions:

Peel the mangoes and wash with water. Cut into thin strips or simply use a vegetable shredder. Wash shallots, garlic, string beans, tomatoes, cilantro and red chili. Chop the tomatoes into halves. Slice shallots into thin strips. Mince red chili and garlic. Trim the Yardlong (string beans) beans and cut into 1-2 inches long.

Using a mortar and pestle, pound the red chili and roasted peanuts with shallots and garlic. Add light soy sauce, coconut palm sugar, lime juice and vegetable oil into the mortar and pestle. Continue beating the ingredients until the spices mix up together.

Get a large mixing bowl and a wooden spoon. Toss the mangoes, beans and tomatoes into the bowl. Add the Thai Salad dressing into the bowl and add some salt to taste. Mix well all ingredients with the dressing. Sprinkle with chopped cilantro. Serves 5-6 persons.

Health Tips:
- Eating green mangoes during summer or hot season will help relieve thirst especially if you add some salt with it. This is due to the ability of mangoes in retaining sodium and iron during hot weather and you perspire more often than normal.

Vegan Pad Thai

Ingredients:

- 400 grams pad Thai noodles
- 4 carrots (julienned)
- 1 large red bell pepper (cut into thin strips)
- 1-2 cups bean sprouts
- 5 cloves garlic (minced)
- 5 green onions (minced)
- 2 tablespoon peanut oil
- ½ cup roasted peanuts (crushed)
- 4 tablespoon vegetable broth
- 6 tablespoon tamari sauce
- 2 teaspoon chili paste
- ½ cup tamarind paste
- 4-5 tablespoon of coconut palm sugar
- 1 tablespoon lime zest
- 1 tablespoon lime juice
- Chopped parsley for garnish

Utensils Needed:

- Large pot (for cooking pad Thai noodles)
- Colander or strainer
- Wok
- Spatula
- Cleaver
- Chopping block
- Mortar and pestle
- Mixing bowl
- Shredder

Directions:

Boil water in a large pot over medium-high heat. Add pad Thai noodles. Cook for 4-5 minutes only. Don't overcook. You will cook the noodles again for about 2-3 minutes in a wok later. Remove water from the noodles using a strainer or colander. Set aside.

Prepare 4 carrots, wash and peel. Cut the carrots using a shredder. Wash bean sprouts and red bell pepper. Cut the tail end of the bean sprouts (dried or black ends). Slice the bell pepper into thin strips using a cleaver. Wash onions and garlic, and then mince. Get a mortar and pestle and pound the roasted peanuts. Save for later use.

Combine tamarind paste, vegetable broth, chili paste, tamari sauce, lime zest and lime juice in a mixing bowl. Mix the liquid mixture thoroughly. Set aside.

Put 2 tablespoon peanut oil in a wok. When the oil is hot, add garlic and onions. Stir-fry until you can smell the aroma of the garlic. Put the vegetables in the wok. Start with carrots, then bell pepper and bean sprouts. Sauté for about 1-2 minutes. Now, add the pad Thai noodles into the wok. Pour the liquid mixture and stir-fry for another 2-3 minutes. Toss all the ingredients with the use of a spatula, and make sure the sauce coats the noodles completely. Sprinkle with roasted peanuts. Garnish with chopped parsley and then serve warm to 4 persons.

Health Tips:
- Roasted peanuts are rich source of Manganese. This mineral assists in bone development and helps you to maintain a healthy bone.

Chickpea Thai Curry

Ingredients:

- 500 grams chickpeas
- 150 grams baby spinach (sliced)
- 3 tablespoon vegetarian red curry paste
- 1 can coconut milk
- 1 large yellow bell paper (julienned)
- 1 large tomato (Cut into thin strips)
- 2 white onion (chopped)
- 3 cloves garlic (peeled and minced)
- 1 teaspoon salt
- 1 teaspoon pepper
- 1 tablespoon rice vinegar
- 2 tablespoon coconut oil

Utensils Needed:

- Saucepan
- Cleaver
- Chopping block
- Spatula

Directions:

Rinse 500 grams of chickpeas and drain. Wash 150 grams of baby spinach and slice into halves. Clean the bell pepper, onion, tomato and garlic. Cut the yellow bell pepper and tomatoes into thin strips. Dice the onion and mince the garlic. Set them aside.

Heat saucepan and add 2 tablespoons of coconut oil. Sauté garlic and onion once oil is hot. Stir in the baby spinach and yellow bell pepper. Add the coconut milk, chickpeas, curry paste and tomatoes. Cover the saucepan and let it simmer. Sprinkle with salt and pepper and add the rice vinegar.

Cook for another 10 minutes and mix occasionally using a spatula. Be careful not to overcook the vegetables. Serve on top of Jasmine rice to 5-6 persons.

Health Tips:
- Chickpea is a good source of non-heme iron. This helps in the production of red blood cells, which is important in distributing oxygen in different organs of the body. Once you eat chickpeas with food rich in vitamin C, non-heme iron is easily absorbed in the body.

Stir-Fry Thai Mixed Vegetables with Garlic Peanut Sauce

Ingredients:

- 150 grams broccoli florets
- 100 grams cucumber (sliced)
- 150 grams cabbage (shredded)
- 150 grams spinach (cut into halves)
- 100 grams celery (cut into 1 – 2 inches long)
- 100 grams bean sprouts
- 2 tablespoon vegetable oil
- ½ cup vegetable broth
- ¼ cup peanut butter
- 5 cloves garlic (minced)
- 1 large onion (minced)
- 3 tablespoon tamari sauce
- 1 red chili (minced)
- Salt to taste

Utensils Needed:

- Wok
- Spatula
- Cleaver
- Chopping Block
- Mortar and Pestle
- Shredder
- Wooden spoon

Directions:

Prepare all the vegetables. Wash with cold water and pat to dry. Cut vegetables into desired shape. Remove dark or dried ends of bean sprouts. Trim the celery and cut into 1-2-inch long. Peel garlic and onion then mince. Cut chili into small pieces. Using a shredder cut the cabbage. Save vegetables for later use.

Get a mortar and pestle, combine garlic, onion and red chili, and then add peanut butter. Pound the ingredients until extracts mix with peanut butter. Pour tamari sauce. Mix using a wooden spoon.

In a wok, heat 2 tablespoons of vegetable oil. Stir-fry the vegetables. Start adding the celery, then broccoli, cabbage, spinach, bean sprouts and cucumber. Season with salt. Sauté until vegetables are tender. Pour ½ cup of vegetable broth. Bring to simmer and then add the peanut garlic mixture and tamari sauce. Stir frequently and wait until sauce thickens. Serve with rice to 5-6 persons.

Health Tips:
- Celery contains substance that helps in reducing blood pressure. Adding celery in your recipe will maintain your blood pressure and lower the risk of heart attacks.
- Bean sprouts can give you an ample source of Vitamin K, which is responsible in blood clotting. When blood clots, it prevents you from any excessive bleeding and promotes healing faster.

Egg-free Thai Corn Fritters (Tod Man Khao Pod)

Ingredients:

- 1 can sweet corn kernel
- ½ cup rice flour
- ½ cup water
- ¼ cup self-rising cornmeal
- 1 tablespoon minced garlic
- 1 tablespoon minced green onion
- Oil for frying
- 1 teaspoon salt
- ½ teaspoon pepper

Utensils Needed:

- Wok
- Spatula
- Cleaver
- Chopping block
- Mixing bowl
- Wooden spoon

Directions:

Clean garlic and green onions with water. Mince the garlic and green onions using a cleaver. Set aside.

In a mixing bowl, combine ¼ cup cornmeal, ½ cup rice flour, minced garlic and green onions. Stir in ½ cup water and sprinkle salt and pepper. Whisk using a wooden spoon until the mixture becomes sticky and firm. Add 1 can or corn kernels and mix well with the mixture.

Prepare a wok and pour oil enough for frying the fritters. When the oils is shimmering and hot. Pour a spoonful of corn mixture into the wok. Flatten with spatula to make it look like a pancake. Cook corn fritters until golden. Make sure to flip occasionally to avoid burning. Place on a tissue covered plate to drain the oil. Serves 4 persons.

Health Tips:
- ◦ Carotenoids enhances vison and prevents you from acquiring macular degeneration according to some studies. This substance is found among yellow fruits and vegetables including corn.

Vegetarian Thai Curry

Ingredients:

- ½ cup sweet potatoes (diced)
- ½ cup carrots (diced)
- ½ cup green beans (cut into 2 inch long)
- ½ cup bamboo shoots (sliced)
- ½ cup mushroom (cut into halves)
- 2 teaspoon light soy sauce
- 3 tablespoon curry paste (Maesri) Any curry brand which has no shrimp or fish
- 3 cloves garlic (minced)
- 2 pieces 2-inch ginger (minced
- 1 can coconut milk
- ¼ cup vegetable broth
- 2 teaspoon coconut palm sugar
- Basil for garnish

Utensils Needed:

- Pot or saucepan
- Ladle
- Cleaver
- Chopping block

Directions:

Wash vegetable with cold water and peel garlic and ginger. Cut each vegetable into desired shape. Mince garlic and ginger. Set them aside.

In a saucepan, over medium heat, pour ¼ cup of vegetable broth. Add garlic and ginger. Place all the vegetables and bring to simmer. Pour 1 can of coconut milk and then mix in curry paste, sugar, and light soy sauce. Cover saucepan and let it boil. Stir from time to time. Cook until vegetables are tender and sauce is thickening. Serve warm on top of rice to 4

persons.

Health Tips:
- If you're pregnant and experiencing morning sickness, eat some ginger and you'll feel more comfortable. Ginger helps in treating motion sickness like nausea, vomiting and dizziness.
- If you want to boost your immune system and fight off against infection and viruses, you better eat some garlic or frequently include it in your recipe. Garlic is a rich source of Vitamin B6, which enhances the ability of the immune system to fight against bacteria.

Grilled Eggplant Thai-Style

Ingredients:

- 1 large eggplant (sliced)
- 2 tablespoon vegetarian oyster sauce
- 3 teaspoon palm sugar
- 1 teaspoon chili sauce
- 2 teaspoon light soy sauce
- 3 small cloves garlic (minced)
- Mint for garnish (chopped)

Utensils Needed:

- Grill
- Large mixing bowl
- Wooden spoon
- Tongs
- Cleaver
- Chopping Block
- Saucepan

Directions:

Prepare one eggplant and 3 cloves of garlic, then wash with water. Slice the eggplant then peel and mince the garlic. Save for later use.

Use a large mixing bowl to combine the sauce for marinating eggplant. Pour 2 tablespoons of vegetarian oyster sauce into the mixing bowl. Add 1 teaspoon of chili sauce and 2 teaspoons of light soy sauce. Mix well. Dissolve 3 teaspoon of palm sugar into the liquid mixture and then put the minced garlic. Stir thoroughly. Get the sliced eggplant and place in the mixing bowl. Let it soak for 1-2 hours.

Grill eggplant slices until it becomes soft and turns

golden. Use a tong to flip the eggplants while grilling to make sure it's evenly grilled. Cook the marinating sauce in a saucepan over medium flame. When sauce is simmering, turn off the stove. Put the eggplants into the saucepan. Carefully combine grilled eggplant with the sauce. Place on a plate and garnish with chopped mint. Serves 2 persons.

Health Tips:
- Mint keeps your respiratory system healthy. It helps in clearing congestion and is good for asthmatic people. It acts as a bronchodilator, which assist in opening the airway and relaxes breathing pattern.

Tofu with Curry Sauce

Ingredients:

- 400 grams tofu (cubed)
- 1 ½ cup coconut milk
- 2 teaspoon curry powder
- 1 tablespoon peanut oil
- 250 grams spinach (sliced)
- 1 large red bell pepper (cut into thin strips)
- 2 cloves garlic (minced)
- 1 onion (minced)
- 1 teaspoon salt
- ½ teaspoon pepper
- 1 teaspoon chopped cilantro (garnish)

Utensils Needed:

- Wok
- Spatula
- Cleaver
- Chopping block

Directions:

Drain tofu and cut into cubes. Wash spinach with water and slice into halves. Clean garlic and onion with water then peel. Mince both garlic and onion, and then cut one red bell pepper into thin slices. Set them aside.

Heat oil in a wok and let it shimmer before putting garlic and onion. Sauté until onion turns translucent. Fry the cubed tofu until golden brown. Be careful when flipping or turning the tofu so it won't break. Add spinach, red bell pepper and 1 and ½ cup coconut milk. Season with curry powder, salt and pepper. Bring to boil. Sprinkle with chopped cilantro then serve warm to 3-4 persons.

Health Tips:
- Tofu has many health benefits. One of this is preventing you to have liver damage. Based on a series of research, tofu has hepatoprotective substance that fights against liver problems.

Coconut Thai Rice

Ingredients:

- 2 cups Jasmine Rice
- 1 cup coconut milk
- 2 cups vegetable broth (low sodium)
- 1/8 teaspoon turmeric
- ¼ teaspoon powdered black pepper
- 1 tablespoon spring onions

Utensils Needed:

- Large pot
- Cleaver
- Chopping Block

Directions:

Wash Jasmine rice with water and rinse well. Wash spring onions and cut into small pieces. Set aside the onions for later use.

Turn your stove into medium high flame. Place a large pot and pour 2 cups of vegetable broth, 1 can of coconut milk, 1/8 teaspoon turmeric, 1/4 teaspoon powdered pepper and 2 cups of jasmine rice. Cover pot and cook until it boils. Turn stove to low heat and cook for 20 minutes until the rice absorbs all the remaining coconut milk and broth. Dash with chopped onions and then serve warm to 4-5 persons.

Health Tips:

- Jasmine rice is popular in Thailand and known as "fragrant rice". It contains a lot of fiber that helps in good digestion and prevents you from having constipation.

Green Papaya Salad (Som Tam)

Ingredients:

- 500 grams green papaya (peeled and shredded)
- 100 grams green beans (cut and pounded)
- 2 tomatoes (sliced)
- 2 cloves garlic (minced)
- 1 large white onion (cut into thin strips)
- 2 tablespoon light soy sauce
- 2 red chili (cut into thin strips)
- 2 tablespoon lime juice
- 1 tablespoon lime zest
- 2 tablespoon coconut palm sugar
- ¼ cup roasted peanuts (crushed)
- 2 tablespoon olive oil

Utensils Needed:

- Mortar and pestle
- Blender
- Large mixing bowl
- Wooden spoon
- Shredder
- Cleaver
- Chopping block

Directions:

Prepare 1 green papaya, peel and cut using a shredder. Wash tomatoes, green beans, garlic, onion and chili, Slice green beans into 2 inches long and cut tomatoes into halves. Mince the garlic and julienne chili and onion. Set them aside.

Mix light soy sauce, lime juice, lime zest sugar and olive oil in the blender. Blend until dressing thickens. Pound green beans, tomatoes, chili, garlic and onion using a mortar and pestle. Now, get a large mixing bowl, combine liquid dressing with the pounded vegetables. Toss the shredded papaya and mix everything thoroughly. Scatter crushed peanuts on top of the salad and serve to 4 persons.

Health Tips:
- Green papaya has a component that helps lactating mother to produce more milk. It is used as a traditional medicine for mothers who have problems in producing milk for their babies.

Vegetarian Thai Noodle Soup

Ingredients:

- ½ cup rice noodle
- 4 cups of vegetable broth
- 200 grams spinach or bok choy (sliced)
- 200 grams carrots (sliced)
- 150 grams zucchini (diced)
- 150 grams green bell pepper (sliced)
- 1 onion (minced)
- 3 cloves garlic (minced)
- 1 Thai red chili (chopped)
- 350 ml coconut milk
- 3 tablespoon light soy sauce
- ½ teaspoon pepper
- ½ teaspoon lime zest
- Cilantro for garnish (chopped)

Utensils Needed:

- Large pot
- Ladle or coconut shell spoon
- Cleaver
- Chopping block
- Strainer or colander

Directions:

Wash al vegetables with cold water. Cut each vegetables into desired shape. Peel the garlic and onion, and then mince. Chop cilantro for garnishing. Save for later use.

Cook noodles in a boiling water, just enough to become slightly tender. Drain noodles using a colander and then set aside.

In a large pot, pour 4 cups of vegetable broth and add mince garlic and ginger. Stir and let it simmer. Add sliced carrots, zucchini, spinach, and green bell pepper. Cover the pot and cook the vegetables until tender. Pour 350 ml of coconut milk into the pot and sprinkle with chopped red chili. Add 3 tablespoon of light soy sauce and sprinkle with pepper and lime zest. Cover pot and bring the soup to simmer. Occasionally mix the soup. Serve with chopped cilantro to 4 persons.

Health Tips:

- Are you feeling sad? Add some green bell peppers in your meal and your mood will definitely change. Green bell pepper contains vitamin B6 that promotes higher production of the hormone serotonin. Serotonin is one of the hormones that keeps you feeling happy and in the mood.

Vegan Thai Steamed Dumplings with Spicy dipping sauce

Ingredients:

- 450 grams pack of vegetarian wonton wrappers
- 100 grams of spinach (sliced)
- 100 grams mushrooms (sliced)
- 100 grams bamboo shoots (chopped)
- 100 grams green bell pepper (chopped)
- 100 grams sweet potato (chopped)
- 100 grams roasted peanuts
- 1 tablespoon lime juice
- 3 cloves garlic (minced)
- 1 onion (minced)
- 2 tablespoon ginger (minced)
- 2 tablespoon rice vinegar
- ¼ cup light soy sauce
- 2 large red chili
- 2 tablespoon spring onions (chopped)

Utensils Needed

- Traditional Bamboo steamer
- Blender
- Mixing bowl
- Wooden spoon

Directions:

Prepare all vegetables. Clean with cold running water and pat to dry. Cut vegetables into small pieces. Now get a blender. Place chopped spinach, mushrooms, bamboo shoots, green bell pepper and potatoes inside the blender. Add roasted peanuts, lime juice, garlic, onion and ginger. Blend all ingredients until mixture are finely chopped. Set aside.

Prepare dipping sauce using a mixing bowl and wooden

spoon. Combine light soy sauce, vinegar, chopped chili and spring onions. Mix well.

Place a spoonful of vegetable mixture at the center of each vegetarian wonton wrappers. Use water to wet all the sides of the wrapper then pull each corner into the center forming a ball. Place dumplings in a bamboo steamer. Steam over high flame for about 20 minutes. Serve with spicy dipping sauce.

Health Tips:

- Potassium keeps your heart healthy and maintains normal blood pressure. This substance is important for the heart to function normally. Bamboo shoots is an excellent source of this vital compound. Including bamboo shoots in your recipe will prevent you from having a heart attack or stroke.

Fried Tofu with Thai Peanut Sauce

Ingredients:

- 400 grams tofu (chopped)
- Vegetable oil enough for frying
- 2 tablespoon cornstarch
- 4 tablespoon flour
- 3 tablespoon light soy sauce
- 4 tablespoon peanut butter
- 2 tablespoon roasted peanuts (crushed)
- 2 tablespoon light vinegar
- 1 tablespoon lime juice
- 2 pieces dried red chili (minced)
- 1 tablespoon coconut palm sugar
- 1 tablespoon chopped coriander
- 3-4 tablespoon water

Utensils Needed:

- Wok
- Spatula
- Cleaver
- Chopping block
- 2 Mixing bowl
- Wooden spoon

Directions:

Prepare 400 grams tofu and drain. Cut into cubes or desired shape. In a mixing bowl, combine flour and cornstarch. Dip cubed tofu into the mixture. Place tofu in a wok with hot vegetable oil. Fry until golden brown.

Get another mixing bowl. Pour 3-4 tablespoon of water with 3 tablespoon of light soy sauce. Dissolve 2 tablespoon of sugar into the mixture. Add 1 tablespoon of lime juice and 2 tablespoon of rice vinegar. Stir continuously. Mix in 4 tablespoon of peanut butter and minced dried chili. Thoroughly whisk sauce with a wooden spoon. Sprinkle with crushed roasted peanuts and chopped coriander.

Serve hot tofu to 4-5 persons with peanut sauce. Enjoy.

Health Tips:
- You like sweets but can't have regular sugar added in your meals. Try coconut palm sugar, which is good for diabetics. This sugar when mix with carbohydrates produces lower glycemic index, which means maintaining normal insulin level in the body.

Pomelo Thai Salad (Yum Som O)

Ingredients:

- 1 large pomelo (chopped and removed skin)
- ½ cup bean sprouts
- 1 red bell pepper (julienned)
- 1 red chili (minced)
- Cilantro for garnish (chopped)
- 1 tablespoon roasted peanuts (garnish)
- 1 onion (minced)
- 1 tablespoon peanut oil
- 2 tablespoon lime juice
- 1 tablespoon lime zest
- 1 tablespoon light soy sauce
- 2 tablespoon coconut palm sugar

Utensils Needed:

- Large mixing bowl
- Wooden spoon
- Mortar and pestle
- Cleaver
- Chopping block

Directions:

Wash pomelo with water and remove the peelings. Carefully cut into cubes. Clean bean sprouts and remove any dried or dark tails from the bean sprouts. Wash red bell pepper and cut into thin strips. Using a mortar and pestle crush the roasted peanuts. Save for later use.

Put 1 tablespoon of peanut oil in a mixing bowl. Combine light soy sauce, lime juice and lime zest. Add sugar, onion and minced red chili. Mix all ingredients well. Toss the pomelo, bean sprouts and red bell pepper into the mixing bowl. Coat the pomelo and the vegetables with the salad dressing.

Sprinkle with chopped cilantro and pounded roasted peanuts. Serves 4 person.

Health Tips:
- Pomelo has high amount of vitamin C, which will help you look young. Vitamin C helps regenerate the cells in the body including skin cells. This slows down the aging process. Eat many pomelos and you will surely look younger than your age.

Stir-Fried Thai Pumpkin Recipe

Ingredients:

- 2 cups pumpkin (diced)
- 1 onion (cut into strips)
- 1 red bell pepper (cut into strips)
- ¼ cup vegetable broth
- 2 tablespoon light soy sauce
- 1 tablespoon brown sugar
- 2 tablespoon vegetable oil
- 1 tablespoon garlic powder
- 1 teaspoon black pepper
- Mint for garnish

Utensils Needed:

- Wok
- Spatula
- Cleaver
- Chopping block

Directions:

Peel the pumpkin after washing with water. Cut into cubes. Wash red bell pepper and onion. Cut red bell pepper into strips and remove the seeds. Peel onions and julienne.

Heat wok over medium flame. Our 2 tablespoon of vegetable oil. Add cubed pumpkins and sprinkle with pepper and garlic powder. Sauté until tender. Pour ¼ cup of vegetable broth, followed by light soy sauce, and sugar. Add onions and red bell pepper into the wok. Bring to simmer until sugar dissolves. Stir-fry occasionally to cook pumpkin well. Garnish with mint and serve to 3 persons.

Health Tips:

- Pumpkin contains both Vitamin A and Vitamin C.

Two essential vitamins to make your immune system stronger. When you eat pumpkin on a daily basis, you prevent yourself from acquiring common colds and bacteria.

Thai Stir-fried Water Spinach (Pad Pak Boong)

Ingredients:

- A bunch of water spinach or water morning glory
- 1 large Thai red chili (julienned)
- 3 cloves garlic (minced)
- 2 tablespoon of vegetarian oyster sauce
- 1 tablespoon of light soy sauce
- 1 tablespoon peanut oil
- 2 teaspoon coconut palm sugar

Utensils Needed:

- Wok
- Spatula
- Cleaver
- Chopping block

Directions:

Clean water spinach with running water. Make sure to remove all the dirt from the stems. Remove the roots and cut into desired length. Slice red chili into thin strips and mince the garlic.

Pour 1 tablespoon of peanut oil into the wok and let it shimmer. Add garlic and then sauté until it turns slightly brown. Put water spinach and chili into the wok. Add vegetarian oyster sauce, light soy sauce and palm sugar. Stir-fry continuously until water spinach is tender. Make sure not to overcook the water spinach. This recipe serves 2-3 persons.

Health Tips:

- Water spinach can help you get a good night sleep and thus resulting to less stress and more comfort. This vegetable has substance that act like sedatives, making you sleepy. Having a well sound sleep helps the body to regain strength and feel more energetic.

Coconut Milk Pudding with Lime

Ingredients:

- 2 cups rice flour
- 4 tablespoon corn flour
- 1 cup coconut milk
- 1 cup coconut cream
- ¼ cup lime juice
- 1 cup coconut palm sugar
- ½ teaspoon salt

Utensils Needed:

- Large mixing bowl
- Small mixing bowl
- Porcelain bowls
- Wooden spoon
- Steamer

Directions:

Prepare topping mixture in a small mixing bowl. Put 2 tablespoon of rice flour and 1 tablespoon of cornstarch in the bowl. Mix in 1 cup of coconut cream and ½ teaspoon of salt. Whisk well. Save for later use.

Place porcelain bowls in a steamer and steam until bowls are hot. While steaming the bowls, prepare the pudding mixture. Get the remaining rice flour and cornstarch and then combine with 1 cup of coconut milk and ¼ cup of lime juice. Mix thoroughly in a large mixing bowl using a wooden spoon. Pour the mixture on the hot porcelain bowls and steam for 15 minutes. Add the topping mixture on top of the pudding and steam for another 5 minutes until topping is soft. Serve warm to 6 persons.

Health Tips:

- Coconut milk helps in losing weight and decreasing appetite. Unlike other milks, which is stored as fats in the body, coconut milk goes directly to the liver after absorption and helps in producing energy for faster metabolism.

Crunchy tofu with Thai Plum Sauce

Ingredients:

- 450 grams tofu (diced)
- 5 tablespoon cornstarch
- 4 tablespoon sesame seeds
- ½ teaspoon salt
- ¼ teaspoon pepper
- 5 tablespoon flour
- 3 tablespoon water
- 4 tablespoon palm sugar
- 3 tablespoon rice vinegar
- 1 tablespoon lime zest
- 5 tablespoon plum jam
- 1 tablespoon red chili (minced)
- 1 tablespoon garlic (minced)
- Vegetable oil for frying
- Parsley for garnish

Utensils Needed:

- Wok
- Spatula
- Mixing bowl
- Wooden spoon
- Clever
- Chopping block

Directions:

Drain and press 450 grams of tofu. Cut tofu into cubes using a cleaver. Wash garlic and red chili and then mince. Save for later use.

In a mixing bowl, whisk together flour, cornstarch, sesame seeds, pepper and salt. Dip the sliced tofu one at a time in the mixing bowl. Fry cubed tofu in a wok with hot vegetable oil. Stir-fry until golden. Place tofu on a plate with paper towels to drain excess oil.

Prepare the plum sauce in a mixing bowl. Combine all

ingredients. Start with mixing liquid ingredients, water, vinegar and plum jam. Then add lime zest, minced red chili, garlic, and palm sugar. Mix everything well.

Heat a wok over medium flame and cook the sauce until it simmer. Place the fried tofu in the wok and toss carefully. Garnish with parsley. Serve warm to 4-5 persons.

Health Tips:
- Eating plums can make your bones healthy. It contains flavonoids and polyphenols, which prevents the bone from deteriorating as you age.

Thai Stir-fried Broccoli florets

Ingredients:

- 500 grams broccoli florets
- 1 large tomato (sliced)
- 1 large onion (julienned)\
- 4 cloves garlic (chopped)
- 2 tablespoon light soy sauce
- 1 tablespoon vegetarian oyster sauce
- 1 tablespoon lime juice
- 1 tablespoon rice vinegar
- 2 teaspoon palm sugar
- 3 tablespoon coconut milk
- 1 teaspoon pepper
- 1 tablespoon olive oil

Utensils Needed:

- Wok
- Spatula
- Cleaver
- Chopping block

Directions:

Wash broccoli, garlic, tomato and onion with water. Cut broccoli into half florets. Chop garlic and cut onions into thins strips. Slice tomato and save vegetables for later use.

Heat wok and add 1 tablespoon of olive oil. Sauté garlic and onion when oil is hot.. Add broccoli florets and tomato. Stir-fry until tender. Pour light soy sauce and vegetarian oyster sauce. Add coconut milk, palm sugar, lime juice and vinegar. Stir-fry every now and then while adding more ingredients. Sprinkle with a teaspoon of pepper. Cook until the vegetables absorb sauce. Serve warm to 4-5 persons.

Health Tips:

- Broccoli is rich of phytonutrients and omega 3 fatty

acids. These anti-inflammatory substances prevent inflammation and swelling. Anti-inflammatory rich food such as Broccoli helps in decreasing adverse effects of chronic diseases.
- According to different studies, broccoli is rich of antioxidants and anti-carcinogen substances that can prevent many types of cancer. This includes gastric, breast, liver and prostate cancer.

Fried Rice Thai-Style with Pineapple and Basil

Ingredients:

- 3 cups of cooked rice
- 3 tablespoon peanut oil
- 2 tablespoon light soy sauce
- 1 tablespoon vegetarian oyster sauce
- 1 tablespoon minced garlic
- 1 tablespoon minced onion
- 1 large red bell pepper (diced)
- 4 tablespoon basil leaves (chopped)
- ½ cup pineapple chunks
- 2 teaspoon curry powder
- ¼ teaspoon pepper

Utensils Needed:

- Wok
- Spatula
- Cleaver
- Chopping block

Directions:

Prepare garlic, onion, basil and red bell pepper. Chop basil leaves and red bell pepper after washing. Wash garlic and onion with water and then peel. Mince them both and then set aside.

Heat 3 tablespoon of peanut oil in a wok. Let oil shimmer and then add minced garlic and onion. Add 3 cups of cooked rice. Stir-fry until chunks or cooked rice are separated into grains. Put light soy sauce, vegetarian oyster sauce and curry powder in the wok. Mix rice with the seasonings. Continuously toss the rice until coated with seasonings. Now, add bell pepper, basil leaves and pineapple chunks. Stir-fry until bell pepper is tender. Sprinkle with powdered pepper and serve warm to 4-5 persons.

Health Tips:
- Sometimes when you cook meals, you get small burns due to shimmering oil. Pineapple contains bromelain that heals those kind of burns. This compound facilitates healing of wounds by decreasing inflammation on the affected area of the skin.

Tofu with Asparagus and Kale in Peanut Curry Sauce

Ingredients:

- 450 grams tofu (cut into small cubes)
- 1 bunch asparagus (cut into 1-2 inch long)
- 1 bunch kale (sliced)
- 1 red bell pepper (sliced)
- 3 tablespoon peanut butter
- 2 teaspoon curry powder
- 2 tablespoon light soy sauce
- 1 tablespoon rice vinegar
- 1 teaspoon pepper
- 1 teaspoon salt
- 2 teaspoon garlic powder
- 1 tablespoon brown sugar
- 3 tablespoon vegetable oil

Utensils Needed:

- Wok
- Spatula
- Mixing bowl
- Wooden spoon
- Cleaver
- Chopping block

Directions:

Drain and cut tofu into small squares. Prepare vegetables and wash with water. Cut 1 red bell pepper and chop asparagus and kale.

Mix sauce in a mixing bowl. Using a wooden spoon, combine light soy sauce, vinegar, and peanut butter. Add dry ingredients. Put a teaspoon of pepper and salt. Mix in curry powder, brown sugar and garlic powder. Whisk thoroughly and then save for later use.

Heat 3 tablespoon of vegetable oil. Once oil is hot, Stir-fry first the tofu until golden. Add asparagus, red bell pepper and kale. Sauté until tender. Pour the peanut sauce into the wok and let it simmer. Toss vegetables and tofu to combine well with the sauce. Serve warm to 4 persons.

Health Tips:
- Having a baby? Eat some kale and you can prevent your babies from getting any birth defects. Kale is a rich source of Folate that assist in brain development and keeps your baby from acquiring abnormalities while still in your womb.

Vegan Thai Coconut Ice Cream

Ingredients:

- 2 cans of coconut milk
- ½ cup sugar
- ¼ cup maple syrup
- ½ teaspoon salt
- 1 loop pandan leaves
- 3 tablespoon cornstarch
- Coconut flakes (toasted)

Utensils Needed:

- Blender
- Wok
- Ladle
- Plastic Container with sealed lid
- Strainer

Directions:

Heat 2 cans of coconut milk in a wok. Add 1 knot of pandan leaves. Stir coconut milk with pandan leaves and bring to simmer. Drain the coconut milk and discard pandan leaves. Set aside and let it cool.

Get a blender. Combine, ¼ cup of maple syrup, ½ cup of sugar, half a teaspoon of salt and 3 tablespoon of cornstarch. Blend until mixture combine. Pour the cooled coconut milk into the blender and blend until mixture becomes thick and smooth. Transfer mixture to a plastic container with sealed airtight lid.

Put the coconut mixture in the freezer. Let it freeze overnight. Serve cold with toasted coconut flakes.

Health Tips:

- Including pandan leaves in your recipe will eliminate stomach cramps and keeps your tummy healthy.
- Maple syrup has Zinc mineral that helps men in

maintaining their prostate strong. In addition, it has Manganese, which promotes increase production of sexual hormones. If you want a healthier reproductive system, then add some maple syrup in your dish.

Carrot Salad Thai-Style

Ingredients:

- 4 carrots (shredded)
- 1 large Thai red chili (minced)
- 1 tablespoon lime zest
- 2 tablespoon lime juice
- 3 tablespoon light soy sauce
- 1 tablespoon garlic (minced)
- 1 tablespoon coconut palm sugar
- 2 tablespoon chopped parsley

Utensils Needed:

- Vegetable shredder
- Cleaver
- Chopping block
- Large mixing bowl
- Wooden spoon

Directions:

Clean carrots u sing cold water. Remove the peelings. Cut into thin strips using a vegetable shredder. Remove the skin of garlic and mince. Coarsely chop parsley. Slice red chili into half and remove the seeds, and then mince. Set them aside.

Prepare a large mixing bowl and wooden spoon for making the carrot salad. Pour 3 tablespoon of light soy sauce and 2 tablespoon of lime juice into the bowl. Whisk well. Dissolve a tablespoon of coconut palm sugar into the liquid mixture. Now, add the shredded carrots, mince garlic, red chili and chopped parsley. Toss using a wooden spoon to coat with the liquid mixture. Sprinkle with 1 tablespoon of lime zest and mix thoroughly. You can put this in the refrigerator or serve right away to 2-3 persons.

Health Tips:
- One of the best natural way of keeping your teeth strong and healthy is eating some carrots. It contains minerals that aids in preventing tooth decay and gum problems.

Tofu and mushroom with Green Curry Paste

Ingredients:

- 400 grams tofu (cubed)
- 1 eggplant (diced)
- 400 grams shiitake mushroom (chopped)
- 4 tablespoon green curry paste
- 1 and ½ cup coconut milk
- 2 tablespoon light soy sauce
- 4 tablespoon of lime zest
- 3 tablespoon of basil leaves (chopped)
- 1 tablespoon of garlic (minced)
- ½ teaspoon salt and pepper
- 3 teaspoon coconut palm sugar

Utensils Needed:

- Saucepan or pot
- Ladle
- Cleaver
- Chopping block

Directions:

Remove excess water from tofu by draining and pressing. Cut carefully using a cleaver on a chopping block. Wash eggplant and mushroom with water and then cut into desired shape. Discard the skin of garlic and mince it. Coarsely cut basil leaves and then set aside.

Heat 1 and ½ cup of coconut milk in a saucepan over medium flame. Add mushroom and eggplant. Mix in light soy sauce, Thai green curry paste, garlic, basil leaves and coconut palm sugar. Cover saucepan and let it boil. Put cubed tofu in the saucepan and lime zest. Season with salt and pepper, and then bring to simmer. Cook for about 2-3 minutes. Serve hot to 4 persons.

Health Tips:
- Shiitake mushroom suppresses tumor mass and prevents cancer cells in developing in your body.

Green Beans with Garlic Tamarind Sauce

Ingredients:

- 500 grams green beans (cut and trimmed)
- 5 garlic cloves (peeled)
- 2 tablespoon vegetable oil
- 1 tablespoon minced onion
- 1 tablespoon tamari sauce
- 3 tablespoon tamarind paste
- 1 tablespoon lime juice
- 2 red chili (chopped)
- 1 teaspoon salt

Utensils Needed:

- Wok
- Spatula
- Cleaver
- Mortar and pestle
- Chopping block

Directions:

Wash green beans with water and trim. Cut into 2 inches long. Remove the garlic skin and using a mortar and pestle pound the garlic cloves. Chop red chili and mince onions. Set them aside.

Heat wok with 2 tablespoon of vegetable oil and then sauté onions and red chili. Add the pounded garlic cloves and green beans. Stir-fry until beans are tender or becomes slightly wilt. Mix tamarind paste, tamari sauce, lime juice and a teaspoon of salt into the wok. Combine all ingredients well. Serves 4-5 persons.

Health Tips:
- Recent research on green beans show that it can prevent formation of colon polyps leading to colon cancer. If you want a healthier colon then better eat some green beans.
- Tamarind is rich of Thiamin, which keeps your muscle tough and your nerves in good function.

Vegetarian Thai Spring Rolls with Sweet peanut sauce

Ingredients:

- 10 pcs rice wrapper
- 1/3 cup carrots (julienned)
- 1/3 cup cabbage (shredded)
- 1/3 cup mushrooms (minced)
- 1/3 cup cucumbers (cut into thin strips)
- 1 bunch spring onions (julienned)
- 1 green bell pepper (cut into thin strips)
- 4 tablespoon of chopped cilantro
- 4 tablespoon of chopped basil
- 1 teaspoon salt
- ½ teaspoon pepper
- 2 tablespoon peanut butter
- 1 tablespoon roasted peanuts (crushed)
- 2 tablespoon palm sugar
- 2 tablespoon light soy sauce
- 1 tablespoon minced garlic
- 1 tablespoon vinegar
- 1 tablespoon peanut oil

Utensils Needed:

- Mortar and pestle
- 1 large mixing bowl
- 1 small mixing bowl
- Wooden spoon
- Baking pan with warm water
- Cleaver
- Chopping block

Directions:

Prepare all the vegetables needed. Wash with cold running water and let it dry. Cut green bell pepper, carrots, and cabbage into thin strips. Chop basil leaves and cilantro. Mince garlic mushroom and green onions.

Combine all vegetables in a large mixing bowl except for garlic. Season with salt and pepper. Toss ingredients with wooden spoon. Set aside.

Get a baking pan and pour some warm water, enough to soak the rice wrappers. Once wrapper is translucent, discard water and let it dry.

Place equal amounts of mixed vegetables on the wrapper. Roll the wrappers and seal completely at the lower end.

For the sauce, mix peanut butter, peanut oil, vinegar, palm sugar, and light soy sauce in a mixing bowl. Sprinkle with roasted peanuts and minced garlic. Serve spring rolls with peanut sauce to 5 persons.

Health Tips:
- Do you want to have a healthier skin, hair and nails? Why not add some cabbage in your meals? Cabbage has high sulfuric content that promotes production of keratin. Keratin is a substance used by many hairstylist, beauty product makers to have smooth, soft and strong hair, nails and skin. Eating cabbage will give you the most natural way of obtaining keratin in your body.

Thai Rice Noodles with Tofu and Mushroom

Ingredients:

- 450 grams rice noodles
- 300 grams tofu (diced)
- 200 grams mushroom (cut into halves)
- 2 tablespoon peanuts (crushed and roasted)
- 1 bunch spring onions (chopped)
- 2 tablespoon Sriracha sauce
- 3 tablespoon vegetable stock
- 4 tablespoon light soy sauce
- 2 tablespoon rice vinegar
- 1 tablespoon lime juice
- 1 tablespoon lime zest
- 2 tablespoon palm sugar
- 1 teaspoon curry powder
- 1 teaspoon salt
- 3 cloves garlic (minced)
- 2 tablespoon basil (chopped)
- 2 tablespoon of vegetable oil

Utensils Needed:

- Wok
- Spatula
- Cleaver
- Chopping block
- Pot
- Strainer

Directions:

Cook 450 grams of rice noodle in a pot of boiling water. Drain noodles and let it dry. Set aside.

Drain and press 300 grams of tofu. Cut into small cubes. Wash mushroom and discard stem. Cut mushroom caps into halves. Wash spring onions and basil, and then pat to dry. Chop into small pieces. Mince garlic and crush peanuts.

Prepare a wok and add 2 tablespoon of vegetable oil. Heat oil until it shimmers. Stir-fry minced garlic and crushed peanuts. When peanuts are roasted, add tofu and sauté until golden. Now, add all the seasonings into the wok; light soy sauce, sriracha sauce, vegetable stock, rice vinegar, palm sugar and lime juice. Now, combine mushroom, spring onions and rice noodles. Stir-fry continuously until mushroom is tender. Sprinkle with lime zest, curry powder and salt. Mix everything well. Serve warm to 3-4 persons.

Health Tips:
- Basil is proven effective in removing kidney stones. It lowers uric acid formation in the body and thus lead to preventing production of stones in the urinary tract system.

Bananas in Coconut Milk

Ingredients:

- 5 large bananas (sliced)
- ½ cup coconut fruit (shredded)
- 1 cup coconut milk
- ½ cup coconut cream
- 1 teaspoon cinnamon
- ½ cup sugar
- a pinch of salt

Utensils Needed:

- Blender
- Mixing bowl
- Cleaver
- Chopping block
- Pot
- Ladle

Directions:

Prepare 1 cup of coconut milk, ½ cup of coconut cream and ½ cup sugar. Pour ingredients in a blender. Blend until mixture consistency is smooth.

Cut 5 pieces banana fruit into small bite sizes. Place bananas in a mixing bowl.

Pour coconut milk mixture in a pot. Cook until it boils. Season with a pinch of salt. Mix well using a ladle.

Get your bowl of bananas and pour hot coconut milk mixture in it. Garnish with 1 teaspoon of cinnamon powder and then serve to 3-4 persons.

Health Tips:

- If you keep on forgetting ingredients when preparing dishes, you just have to eat more bananas. Bananas has a compound called tryptophan, which enhances your memories.
- Cinnamon lowers the bad cholesterol in your body while increases the good cholesterol. This means that if you add a pinch of cinnamon in your recipe, you reduces your risk of having stroke and heart attack.

Asparagus with Spicy Curry Sauce

Ingredients:

- 450 grams asparagus (cut into 2-3 inches long)
- 1 large onion (chopped)
- 4 cloves garlic (minced)
- 3 tablespoon Sriracha Sauce
- 2 tablespoon light soy sauce
- 1 teaspoon lime juice
- 2 teaspoon curry powder
- 2 tablespoon peanut oil
- 1 teaspoon salt
- ½ teaspoon pepper
- 2 Thai red chili (minced)
- 2 teaspoon palm sugar

Utensils Needed:

- Wok
- Spatula
- Cleaver
- Chopping block
- Mixing bowl
- Wooden spoon

Directions:

Clean asparagus with cold water. Snap off the tough ends of asparagus and cut into 2-3 inches long. Wash onions, garlic and red chili, and then mince.

Combine your spicy curry sauce in a mixing bowl. Add Sriracha sauce, light soy sauce, lime juice, and palm sugar. Whisk until sugar dissolves in liquid mixture. Mix in the curry powder and minced red chili. Set aside for later use.

Prepare your wok. Put 2 tablespoon of peanut oil. Once it shimmers, add garlic and onion. Wait until onion turns transparent before adding the asparagus. Sauté until asparagus is tender. Now, pour your spicy curry sauce into the wok and stir-fry. Season with a teaspoon of salt and half a teaspoon of pepper. Cook for just 1-2 minutes then serve warm to 3-4 persons.

Health Tips:
- If you have diabetes mellitus, a lifestyle disease that inhibits you from taking large amount of sugar. Make sure to include onions in your dishes. Onions have a substance called Chromium that controls normal blood sugar in the body.

Celery Creamy Coconut Soup

Ingredients:

- 400 grams celery (cut into small pieces)
- 1 cup coconut milk
- 1 cup coconut cream
- ¼ cup vegetable broth
- 1 bunch spring onions (chopped)
- 2 teaspoon lime zest
- 2 teaspoon lime juice
- ½ teaspoon pepper
- 1 teaspoon garlic powder
- 1 teaspoon ginger powder

Utensils Needed:

- Pot
- Ladle
- Cleaver
- Chopping block

Directions:

Trim celery after washing with water. Cut into small pieces. Wash a bunch of spring onions and chop. Save celery and onions for later use.

Turn oven into medium flame. Place a large pot and pour 1 cup of coconut milk with 1 cup of coconut cream. Mix in ¼ cup of vegetable broth. Cover the pot and let it boil. Now, add minced celery and spring onions. Sprinkle with lime zest, garlic and ginger powder. Add lime juice and season with pepper. Bring to simmer. Serve hot to 4 persons.

Health Tips:

- Celery contains great amount of sodium and potassium. These electrolytes are important to maintain the normal pumping mechanism of your heart. Furthermore, potassium and sodium keeps the cells in body well hydrated.

Tofu Satay with Spicy Peanut Sauce

Ingredients:

- 500 grams tofu (cut into rectangular shape)
- 1 onion (minced)
- 3 cloves garlic (minced)
- 2 inches galangal (minced)
- 3 tablespoon lemon grass (minced)
- 1 teaspoon turmeric powder
- 1 teaspoon cumin powder
- 2 tablespoon vegetable oil
- ½ teaspoon salt
- ¼ teaspoon pepper
- 1 tablespoon palm sugar
- 3 tablespoon light soy sauce
- 3 tablespoon coconut milk
- 2 teaspoon lime juice
- 4 tablespoon peanut butter
- 1 tablespoon roasted peanut (crushed)
- 2 teaspoon lime juice
- 1 tablespoon light soy sauce
- 3 red chili (minced)
- 1 tablespoon palm sugar
- 2 tablespoon coconut cream

Utensils Needed:

- Griller
- Cleaver
- Chopping block
- 2 mixing bowl
- Bamboo skewers
- Lemongrass Brush

Directions:

Prepare 500 grams of tofu, drain and press excess water. Cut into rectangular shape. Set aside.

Combine Satay marinate sauce in a large mixing bowl. Put minced garlic, lemongrass, galangal and onion in the bowl. Mix in 3 tablespoon of coconut milk, light soy sauce and lime juice. Add palm sugar, vegetable oil, turmeric powder, and cumin powder. Sprinkle with salt and pepper. Whisk the marinate sauce until it combines completely. Soak tofu in the bowl. Cover the bowl and place in the refrigerator. Marinate for half a day or overnight.

Prepare your spicy peanut sauce. In a mixing bowl, pour coconut cream, light soy sauce, lime juice and peanut butter. Stir until liquid mixture combines. Add minced red chili and palm sugar. Mix well and then sprinkle with crushed peanuts.

Get your marinated tofu and thread it to a bamboo skewer. Heat your griller and grill until golden on both sides. You can paint the tofu with the marinate sauce using a lemongrass brush while grilling. Serve warm to 5-6 persons with spicy peanut sauce.

Health Tips:
- Galangal is a close relative of ginger and native to Thailand. An herbal plant that you can use for treating diarrhea. It promotes good digestion as well.

Cucumber Salad Thai-Style

Ingredients:

- 3 large cucumbers (sliced)
- 4 tablespoon lime juice
- 1 tablespoon lime zest
- 2 tablespoon peanut oil
- 2 tablespoon peanuts (pounded)
- 1 tablespoon red chili (minced)
- 2 tablespoon coconut palm sugar
- 1 bunch green onion (minced)
- 1 teaspoon salt

Utensils Needed:

- Mortar and pestle
- Large mixing bowl
- Cleaver
- Chopping block
- Wooden spoon

Directions:

Clean cucumber and let it dry. Cut into desired shape or thinly slice using a cleaver. Mince red chili and set aside.

Pound peanuts using mortar and pestle. Then, crushed minced red chili. Pour 4 tablespoon of lime juice and sprinkle with lime zest. Pound to combine ingredients. Transfer mixture into a large mixing bowl. Add palm sugar and season with salt. Toss sliced cucumbers and mix well with the salad dressing. Serves 2-3 persons.

Health Tips:

- Cucumbers are one of the best replacement for water

that can provide you with many nutrients. It's consist of 95% water and has great amount of vitamin B and C, which make enhances your brain function and keeps you away from infection.

Stir-Fry Mushroom and Basil Curry

Ingredients:

- 500 grams mushroom (shiitake or Portobello)
- 5 tablespoon basil leaves (coarsely chopped)
- 2 tablespoon vegetable oil
- 4 cloves garlic (minced)
- 1 onion (minced)
- 2 inches ginger (minced)
- 3 tablespoon light soy sauce
- 1 tablespoon lime juice
- 1/4 teaspoon turmeric powder
- ½ teaspoon curry powder

Utensils Needed:

- Wok
- Cleaver
- Chopping block
- Spatula

Directions:

Wash mushroom and discard the stem. Cut caps into halves. Clean basil leaves and coarsely chop into small pieces or cut into thin strips. Was onion, garlic and ginger with water, and then peel the skin. Mince after removing the peeling. Set aside.

Heat 2 tablespoon of vegetable oil in a wok. Sauté garlic, ginger and onion. Once onion is translucent, add the cut mushrooms. Stir-fry and combine all ingredients until mushroom turns golden in color. Pour 3 tablespoon of light soy sauce and a tablespoon of lime juice. Put the chopped basil leaves and mix well. Sprinkle with turmeric and curry powder. Toss all ingredients together. Serve warm to 5 persons.

Health Tips:

- Turmeric has strong anti-inflammatory effects on the body. This is why turmeric can ease pain naturally. Just adding this to your dishes will keep you away from getting any diseases that is caused by inflammation.

Hot and Spicy Peanut Fried Rice

Ingredients:

- 4 cups cooked rice
- 2 tablespoon peanut oil
- 100 grams tofu (cubed)
- 1 large onion (sliced)
- 4 cloves garlic (minced)
- 1 large red bell pepper (julienned)
- 100 grams cabbage (shredded)
- 100 grams carrot (julienned)
- 2 tablespoon cilantro (coarsely chopped)
- 1 cup peanut butter
- ¼ cup roasted peanuts (crushed)
- 3 tablespoon tamari sauce
- 1 tablespoon light soy sauce
- 2 tablespoon lime juice
- 1 tablespoon lime zest
- 1 teaspoon curry powder
- 1 teaspoon chili powder

Utensils Needed:

- Wok
- Spatula
- Cleaver
- Chopping block
- Large mixing bowl
- Wooden spoon
- Mortar and pestle

Directions:

Prepare 100 grams of carrot, cabbage and tofu, and 1 large red bell pepper. Cut into desired shape after washing with water. Peel garlic and onion and then mince. Chop cilantro leaves and save for later use. Pound peanuts using a mortar and pestle and then set aside.

Combine peanut butter, tamari sauce, light soy sauce, lime juice and lime zest in a mixing bowl. Add crushed peanuts, curry, and chili powder into the mixture. Whisk using a wooden spoon to mix ingredients.

Put 2 tablespoon of peanut oil in a wok and heat over medium flame. Add garlic and onion and then slowly add strips of carrot, red bell pepper, cubed tofu and shredded cabbage. Pour the peanut sauce into the wok and stir until all ingredients combine. Slowly add the cooked rice and stir-fry continuously to avoid rice clumping. Sprinkle with chopped cilantro and serve warm to 5-6 persons.

Health Tips:
- Cilantro is a natural detoxifying herb that cleanse the body from accumulated toxic metals like mercury and aluminum. It has chemical substances, which bind these toxins and get them out of the body.

Mango Thai Pudding

Ingredients:

- 4 ripe mangoes (sliced)
- 2 cups coconut milk
- 6 tsp gelatin
- 1 cup water
- 1 cup coconut palm sugar
- 10 mint leaves (minced)
- Mint leaves for garnish
- 2 teaspoon lime zest

Utensils Needed:

- Blender or food processor
- Sauce pan
- Ladle
- Cleaver
- Chopping block
- Mixing bowl

Directions:

Wash 4 ripe mangoes and peel. Cut into small chunks and discard seed. Save ¼ cup for garnishing. Chop mint leaves and save for later use.

In a food processor or blender. Add small chunks of mangoes and crushed mint leaves. Season with 2 teaspoon of lime zest and pour 2 cups of coconut milk then blend until smooth. Set aside.

Heat 1 cup of water in a sauce pan. Transfer to a mixing bowl. Sprinkle 6 teaspoon of gelatin into the bowl while stirring. Now, dissolve 1 cup of coconut palm sugar into the mixture. Continue mixing the gelatin mixture. Pour the mixture into the food processor with pureed mangoes and then blend until completely smooth. Put the pudding in a mold or bowl, then refrigerate for a couple of hours or overnight. Garnish with mint leaves and small chunks of mangoes on top and then serve to 5-6 persons.

Health Tips:
- Are you having a hard time and feels stressed? Mint is a natural stimulant that helps you to get in your mood and increases your energy. Including mint in your dishes will help you to work well and do your activities daily with more enthusiasm.

Spicy Ginger Soup with Coconut Milk

Ingredients:

- ½ cup ginger (minced)
- 2 cups coconut milk
- ½ cup coconut cream
- ¼ cup vegetable broth
- 2 tablespoon lime juice
- 1 tablespoon lime zest
- 1 teaspoon cumin powder
- 2 garlic cloves (minced)
- Basil for garnish
- 2 teaspoon coconut palm sugar
- 1 medium size onion (minced)
- 1 teaspoon salt

Utensils Needed:

- Pot
- Ladle
- Cleaver
- Chopping block

Directions:

Peel ginger, onion and garlic after washing with water. Mince all vegetables and then set aside.

Boil 2 cups of coconut milk in a pot over medium heat. Add ½ cup of coconut cream, ¼ cup of vegetable broth and 2 tablespoon of lime juice. Put ginger, garlic and onion in the pot and cover. Add coconut palm sugar and then bring to simmer. Reduce heat to low. Sprinkle with 1 tablespoon of lime zest, 1 teaspoon of cumin powder and a teaspoon of salt. Stir occasionally to combine ingredients. Garnish with chopped basil leaves and serve warm to 3 persons.

Health Tips:

- If you are suffering from simple respiratory illnesses

to complex problem of the respiratory system like asthma, better add cumin into your meals and you will relieve yourself from these problems. The anti-inflammatory compound in cumin clears airway of any mucus accumulation. It also prevents constriction of your airways to prevent you from any asthma attacks.

Broccoli and Cauliflower Sweet Curry

Ingredients:

- 400 grams broccoli florets
- 400 grams cauliflower florets
- 2 teaspoon curry powder
- 4 tablespoon coconut palm sugar
- ½ cup coconut milk
- 1 onion (minced)
- 3 cloves garlic (minced)
- 1 teaspoon salt
- ½ teaspoon pepper
- Cilantro for garnish
- 2 tablespoon vegetable oil
- 1 tablespoon light soy sauce

Utensils Needed:

- Wok
- Spatula
- Cleaver
- Chopping block

Directions:

Wash broccoli, cauliflower, onion and garlic with cold water. Pat to dry then cut broccoli and cauliflower into florets. You may cut florets into halves. Mince garlic and onion, then set aside.

Prepare a wok and put 2 tablespoon of vegetable oil. When oil is shimmering and hot, sauté garlic and onion until onion turns transparent. Add broccoli and cauliflower florets and stir-fry until tender. Pour coconut milk, light soy sauce and add palm sugar, then bring to simmer. Season with curry powder, salt and pepper. Serve warm with chopped cilantro to 6 persons.

Health Tips:
- Cauliflower contains Glucoraphanin, a compound that stops fat buildup in the blood vessels of your heart. This ensures good circulation of blood in the heart and prevents you from getting any serious cardiovascular problem.

Stir-Fry Sweet and Sour Potato Curry

Ingredients:

- 500 grams potato (peeled and cubed)
- 1 large onion (minced)
- 3 cloves garlic (minced)
- ¼ cup coconut milk
- 2 tablespoon coconut palm sugar
- 1 tablespoon rice vinegar
- 2 teaspoon lime juice
- 1 teaspoon lime zest
- 2 teaspoon curry powder
- 1 teaspoon salt
- 2 tablespoon vegetable oil
- Parsley for garnish

Utensils Needed:

- Wok
- Spatula
- Cleaver
- Chopping block
- Pot of water
- Strainer

Directions:

Wash potatoes and peel. Boil a pot of water and add potatoes. Partially cook the potatoes then discard water using a strainer. Pat to dry and cut into cubes. Set aside. Mince garlic and onion after washing, then save for frying.

Turn stove into medium flame. Put wok and add 2 tablespoon of vegetable oil. Once oil is hot, add minced garlic and onion. Mix in the cubed potatoes and stir-fry until tender. Pour ¼ cup of coconut milk into the wok. Add lime juice and rice vinegar. Stir frequently. Season with salt, curry powder and lime zest. Toss all ingredients to mix well. Garnish with chopped parsley and serve to 2 persons.

Health Tips:
- If you're not getting enough sunlight and you still want to have adequate amount of Vitamin D in your body. You should eat more potatoes. Potato is a rich source of D vitamins, which helps in calcium absorption. Calcium promotes bone development and keeps your bone healthy and strong.

Carrot Noodles with Tofu in Creamy Peanut Sauce

Ingredients:

- 7 carrots (julienned or cut into long thin strips)
- 250 grams tofu (diced)
- 1 large red bell pepper (sliced)
- 1 small eggplant (cut into strips)
- 3 tablespoon peanuts (roasted and crushed)
- ¼ cup peanut butter
- ½ cup coconut milk
- ½ cup coconut cream
- 2 teaspoon curry powder
- 2 tablespoon lime juice
- 4 cloves garlic (minced)
- 2 tablespoon light soy sauce
- 2 tablespoon peanut oil
- 1 large onion (minced)
- 1 tablespoon chopped cilantro

Utensils Needed:

- Wok
- Spiralizer or shredder
- Spatula
- Chopping block
- Cleaver
- Mixing bowl
- Wooden spoon

Directions:

Wash all vegetables in cold running water. Then pat to dry. Using a shredder or spiralizer, cut carrots after peeling. Mince garlic and onion. Slice eggplant and red bell pepper and then set aside. Drain tofu of any excess water. Cut into cubes.

In a mixing bowl, combine ingredients for peanut

sauce. Put ¼ cup of peanut butter, with ½ cup of coconut milk and ½ cup of coconut cream. Add light soy sauce and lime juice. Mix the mixture until smooth. Now, add minced garlic, onion and chopped cilantro. Save for later use.

Heat wok with 2 tablespoon of peanut oil. Sauté tofu and crushed peanuts until golden, then add carrot noodles, eggplant and bell pepper. Stir-fry until tender. Pour the creamy peanut sauce into the wok and continuously toss all the ingredients. Cook for about 2-3 minutes, then serve to 6 persons.

Health Tips:
- Carrots are well known great source of Vitamin A. It contains Beta-Carotene, which keeps your skin healthy and maintains a good and clear eyesight.
- Eating eggplants can boost your cognitive abilities. It has rich amount of phytonutrients that enhances your brain cells.

Thai Tomato Salad

Ingredients:

- 500 grams tomatoes (sliced)
- A bunch of spring onions (chopped)
- 2 medium size white onions (cut into thin strips)
- 1 tablespoon lime juice
- 1 tablespoon of rice vinegar
- 2 teaspoon lime zest
- 2 teaspoon palm sugar
- 1 teaspoon salt
- ¼ teaspoon pepper

Utensils Needed:

- Mixing bowl
- Wooden spoon
- Cleaver
- Chopping block

Directions:

Prepare 500 grams of tomatoes and slice into desired shape after washing with water. Wash white and green onions with water. Cut white onions into thins strips, while mince the green onions.

In a mixing bowl, put a tablespoon of lime juice and a tablespoon of rice vinegar. Dissolve 2 teaspoon of palm sugar into the liquid ingredients. Sprinkle with lime zest, salt and pepper. Whisk salad dressing using a wooden spoon. Toss tomatoes, green and white onions into the bowl and coat completely with the dressing. Serve right away to 3-4 persons.

Health Tips:

- Tomatoes are good natural diuretic due to high water content. This means, you can easily urinate more often when eating tomatoes. Removing toxins out of the body through urinating prevents you from acquiring certain urinary tract problems or even kidney diseases.

Fried Chive Cake Thai-Style (Kanom Gui Chai)

Ingredients:

- 150 grams chives (minced)
- 2 cloves garlic (minced)
- ¼ teaspoon baking soda
- ¾ cup glutinous rice flour
- ¼ cup tapioca flour
- ¾ cup water
- ¼ teaspoon salt
- ¼ teaspoon pepper
- 3 tablespoon tamari sauce
- 1 tablespoon light soy sauce
- 1 tablespoon lime juice
- 1 tablespoon rice vinegar
- 1 tablespoon palm sugar
- 3 tablespoon vegetable oil
- 2 red chili (minced)

Utensils Needed:

- Steamer
- Wok
- Spatula
- Baking pan
- Cleaver
- Chopping block
- Mixing bowls
- Wooden spoon

Directions:

Wash chives and garlic with water, then mince. Put minced chives and garlic in a mixing bowl. Season with salt and pepper, then mix. Set aside.

Get a large mixing bowl; sift rice flour, tapioca flour and baking soda into the bowl. Add ¾ cups of water and whisk.

Combine chives mixture and rice flour mixture together. Stir using a wooden spoon until smooth. Transfer mixture in a baking pan. Steam for about 20-25 minutes until chive cake turns transparent. Let it cool.

Prepare your dipping sauce. Add tamari sauce, light soy sauce, rice vinegar and lime juice in a mixing bowl. Sprinkle with minced red chili and mix well with the liquid sauce. Save for later use.

Cut the chive cakes into desired shape and prepare for frying. Heat 3 tablespoon of vegetable oil in a wok. When oil shimmers, Stir-fry chive cakes until golden on both sides. Place on a plate covered with paper towel to drain excess oil. Serve warm with dipping sauce to 4 persons.

Health Tips:

- Chive has great amount of compound that lowers your risk of developing cardiovascular diseases. It contains potassium, which helps in maintaining normal pumping action of the heart. It has allicin and quercetin substances that reduces bad cholesterol level in your body. This prevents accumulation of plaque in your blood vessels. Eating chives, will keep your heart healthy and strong.

Bitter Gourd with Garlic and Peanut Sauce

Ingredients:

- 450 grams bitter gourd (sliced and seeded)
- 2 tablespoon vegetable oil
- 2 tablespoon peanuts (roasted and pounded)
- 5 cloves garlic (minced)
- 2 shallots (minced)
- 2 tablespoon light soy sauce
- 2 tablespoon peanut butter
- 1 tablespoon lime juice
- 1 tablespoon lime zest
- 1 teaspoon salt
- ½ teaspoon pepper

Utensils Needed:

- Wok
- Spatula
- Cleaver
- Chopping block
- Mortar and pestle
- Mixing bowl
- Wooden spoon

Directions:

Prepare 450 grams bitter gourd and wash with cold water. Cut into halves and remove the seeds. Slice thinly about ½ an inch thick. Clean shallots and garlic with water and remove the peeling. Mince using a cleaver and then set aside.

Pound peanuts using a mortar and pestle. Transfer to a mixing bowl and combine with peanut butter. Add 2 tablespoon of light soy sauce, 1 tablespoon of lime juice and a tablespoon of lime zest. Mix well.

Turn stove into medium flame and heat 2 tablespoon of vegetable oil in a wok. Once oil is hot, add garlic and shallots. Sauté until you can smell the aroma of the minced garlic. Stir-fry bitter gourd until tender. Add peanut sauce mixture and bring to simmer. Season with salt and pepper and stir continuously to cook evenly. Serve warm to 3-4 persons.

Health Tips:
- Bitter gourd contains a compound that helps the liver to function well and treats underlying liver problems. It also promotes good digestion and enhances bladder function.

Stir-fried Sweet and Spicy Brussel Sprout

Ingredients:

- 500 grams Brussel sprouts (cut into halves)
- 3 cloves garlic minced
- 2 tablespoon vegetable oil
- 2 tablespoon tamari soy sauce
- 1 tablespoon light soy sauce
- 1 tablespoon rice vinegar
- 2 tablespoon coconut palm sugar
- 3 Thai red chili (minced)

Utensils Needed:

- Wok
- Spatula
- Cleaver
- Chopping block

Directions:

Rinse Brussel sprouts with lukewarm water and remove any dark or yellowish parts. Cut into halves. Remove garlic husk and mince. Wash red chili with water and cut into small pieces. Set them aside.

Prepare a wok and heat 2 tablespoon of vegetable oil. Sauté garlic until golden. Add minced Thai red chili and stir well. Toss 500 grams of Brussel sprouts in the wok and stir-fry until brown on both sides. Pour tamari soy sauce, light soy sauce, and rice vinegar into the wok. Combine all ingredients to coat Brussel sprouts thoroughly with seasonings. Add coconut palm sugar and bring to simmer. Stir-fry frequently to avoid over cooking. Serve warm to 4-5 persons.

Health Tips:

- Cooking Brussel sprouts well is the key to get the

nutrients that help fights against cancer. It contains glucosinolates, sulforaphane and isothiocyanates. These compounds are responsible for protecting you from getting free radicals that damage the cells in your body leading to different forms of cancer.

Sweet Taro Balls in Creamy Coconut Milk

Ingredients:

- 1 ½ cup taro
- 2 cups glutinous rice flour
- 4 tablespoon tapioca flour
- 1 cup coconut milk
- 1 cup coconut cream
- 5 tablespoon coconut milk (for taro balls dough)
- ¼ teaspoon salt
- Water for steaming taro
- 1 cup coconut palm sugar
- ¼ cup grated coconut fruit

Utensils Needed:

- Steamer
- Fork for mashing taro
- Pot
- Ladle
- Shredder
- Mixing bowl
- Wooden spoon

Directions:

Rinse taro with cold water to remove dirt. Steam until soft and peel the skin. Mash taro using a fork. Transfer in a mixing bowl. Add rice flour, tapioca flour and ¼ teaspoon of salt in the bowl. Whisk until combine. Pour 4 tablespoon of coconut milk into the bowl, one tablespoon at a time while stirring. Knead the taro dough and form into balls. Set them aside.

In a pot, boil 1 cup of coconut milk and a cup of coconut cream. When milk is boiling, add the taro balls. Dissolve 1 cup of palm sugar and stir using a ladle to mix all ingredients well. When taro balls float to the surface of the coconut milk, add shredded coconut fruit. Bring to simmer and serve warm to 6 persons.

Health Tips:
- Taro is rich of vitamins A and E, which enhances vision and promotes smooth and healthy skin. Eating this fruit will prevent you from getting eye diseases and assists in healing wounds faster, making your skin blemish free.

Sautéed Bean Sprouts with Tofu

Ingredients:

- 500 grams bean sprouts
- 250 grams tofu (cubed)
- A bunch of chives (cut into strips)
- 1 tablespoon parsley (minced)
- 2 cloves garlic (minced)
- 2 tablespoon light soy sauce
- 1 teaspoon curry powder
- ½ teaspoon salt
- 1 teaspoon coconut palm sugar
- 2 tablespoon peanut oil

Utensils Needed:

- Wok
- Spatula
- Cleaver
- Chopping block

Directions:

Wash bean sprouts with cold water and snap off the tail. Pat to dry. Drain and cut tofu into cubes. Rinse chives and cut into 2 inches strips. Peel garlic and mince.

Prepare a wok. Pour 2 tablespoon of peanut oil and heat until oil shimmers. Add garlic and tofu. Stir-fry until brown and then add the bean sprouts. Now, add chives and parsley, then pour light soy sauce into the wok. Sprinkle with curry powder, salt and palm sugar. Stir-fry to combine seasonings. Toss until bean sprouts are crispy. Serve warm to 4-6 persons.

Health Tips:

- Iron is important in the body for blood circulation and for healthy red blood cells, which carry oxygen throughout the body. Parsley is a good source of iron that prevents you from iron deficiency anemia, a disease that happens when not enough red blood cells are present in the body. Adding parsley in your recipe will give you more iron and thus leading to healthier red blood cells.

Thai Cassava Dessert with Coconut Milk

Ingredients:

- 500 grams cassava (cut into small bite size pieces)
- ½ cup coconut milk
- ½ cup coconut cream
- 3 cups water
- ½ cup coconut palm sugar
- 2 tablespoon tapioca flour
- ¼ teaspoon salt
- 1 tablespoon lime zest
- Sesame seeds for garnish

Utensils Needed:

- Saucepan
- Ladle
- Cleaver
- Chopping block

Directions:

Peel the hard skin of 500 grams cassava and rinse thoroughly with water. Cut the root ends. Slice into small bite sizes.

In a saucepan over medium heat, pour 3 cups of water. Add a tablespoon of lime zest and half a cup of palm sugar. Put 500 grams of cassava and cover the pan. Boil and cook until cassava is soft and caramelized. Stir occasionally. Transfer to small bowls. Set aside.

Prepare a mixture of coconut milk, coconut cream, ¼ teaspoon of salt and 2 tablespoon of tapioca flour in a saucepan. Bring to boil. Pour the coconut milk sauce using a ladle in the bowls of cassava with sesame seeds on top. Serve warm to

4 persons.

Health Tips:
- Cassava is gluten-free and this means, it's vegan and healthy. Certain illnesses like celiac disease will benefit in eating cassava. If you want a good substitute for rice product, cassava will suit your recipe needs.

Orange Carrot Soup Thai-Style

Ingredients:

- 3 large carrots (diced)
- 1 cup orange zest
- 1 tablespoon lime zest
- 2 tablespoon tamarind paste
- 3 tablespoon light soy sauce
- 2 inches galangal (minced)
- 1 teaspoon salt
- 1 tablespoon coconut palm sugar
- ½ teaspoon pepper
- 2 minced red chili (garnish)
- 1 tablespoon peanuts (garnish)
- 1 tablespoon coriander (garnish)

Utensils Needed:

- Food processor
- Pot
- Ladle
- Cleaver
- Chopping block

Directions:

Clean carrots and peel the skin. Pat to dry using a cloth and cut into small pieces. Mince galangal and set aside.

Put diced carrots in a food processor. Add 1 cup of orange juice, and a tablespoon of lime zest. Blend until pureed. Transfer mixture into a pot.

Turn stove on medium flame. Heat carrot and orange mixture. Add minced galangal, minced chili and tamarind paste and light soy sauce. Stir until ingredients combine. Dissolve a tablespoon of coconut palm sugar and sprinkle with salt and pepper. Cover the pot and bring to boil. Sprinkle with coriander and peanuts. Serve hot to 4 persons.

Health Tips:
- Orange is one of the citrus fruits that has a lot of vitamin C. Consuming oranges means helping your body to fight against common colds, viruses and even cancer.
- It also contains hesperidin, which slows down tumor growth in the body and thus promoting cancer cell death, leaving your body virtually cancer free.

Thai Sweet and Sour Tofu

Ingredients:

- 500 grams tofu (cubed)
- 1 large red bell pepper (diced)
- 1 large green bell pepper (diced)
- 2 cloves garlic (minced)
- 1 large onion (sliced)
- 3 tablespoon vegetable oil
- 2 tablespoon tamarind paste
- 1 tablespoon lime juice
- 3 tablespoon coconut palm sugar
- 1 tablespoon light soy sauce
- 1 tablespoon rice vinegar
- 1/2 teaspoon cayenne powder
- ½ teaspoon salt

Utensils Needed:

- Wok
- Spatula
- Cleaver
- Chopping block
- Mixing bowl
- Wooden spoon

Directions:

Drain 500 grams tofu of any excess water by pressing. Cut into cubes and set aside. Wash bell peppers, garlic and onion with water. Mince garlic and onion and then dice the green and red bell pepper. Save for later use.

In a mixing bowl, prepare a sweet and sour sauce. Add tamarind paste, lime juice and rice vinegar in the bowl. Mix in the coconut palm sugar. Stir well.

Heat 3 tablespoon of vegetable oil and stir-fry garlic, onions and tofu. Sauté until tofu becomes crispy and turns brown on both side. Add red and green bell pepper and pour light soy sauce into the wok. Now, put the sweet and sour sauce. Sprinkle with salt and cayenne powder and toss all ingredients to coat the tofu. Serve warm to 4-5 persons.

Health Tips:
- Cayenne powder makes dishes spicy and hot, but it promotes good digestion and relieves stomach pain. It also helps treat diarrhea and irregular bowel movements. Adding this spice in your meal keeps your tummy strong.

CONCLUSION

I give thanks for being able to share these love-filled recipes with you, your friend and family. I hope you try each one and share your experience. I will be creating books and more to express our way of eating to the world. Please look for more in the future.

EAT, LOVE, SMILE, LAUGH, SHARE AND **COOK!!!!**

Thank you

Vege-Thai-Rian

Ariya Netjoy Presents:

VEGANIZED

CHINESE HEALTHY COOKING

Buddha's Way

BE GOOD AND KIND TO ALL LIVING BEINGS

PACTICE IT

Copyrights 2017 All rights reserved © Ariya Netjoy

No part of this publication or the information in it may be quoted from or reproduced in any form by means such as printing, scanning, photocopying, or otherwise without prior written permission of the copyright holder.

Sunny Thai Publishing

Terms of Use Disclaimer Efforts have been made to ensure that the information in this book is accurate. However, the author and the publisher do not hold any responsibility for errors, omissions, or contrary interpretation of the subject matter herein. The recipes provided in this book are for informational purposes only and are not intended to provide dietary advice. A medical practitioner should be consulted for dietary advice. Additionally, recipe cooking times may require adjustment depending on age and quality of appliances and tools. Readers are urged to take all needed precautions to ensure ingredients are fully cooked to avoid the dangers of foodborne illnesses. The author and publisher do not take any responsibility for any consequences that may result due to following the instructions provided in this book.

Be sure to look for our other books available on Amazon.

Thank you for being a loyal reader and friend. As a reward, we would like to bring even more delicious vegan and vegetarian dishes into your life, FREE! All you have to do, is sign up with your email and you are set. Everything is free and full of fun so come on and eat with us! Click the blue mail above. Available on the Kindle Version

Table of Contents

INTRODUCTION
Spicy Stir-Fried Eggplant with Snap Beans
Steamed Baby Bok Choy with Shiitake Mushroom sauce
Stir-fried Broccoli with Sesame Garlic Sauce
Sesame Ginger Noodles with Steamed Tofu and Broccoli
Chinese Vegan Peanut Soup
Sweet and Sour Onion Side Dish
Spicy Steamed Spinach and Bean Sprout Salad
Fried Tofu with Veggies
Steamed Wonton Veggies
Stir fry Spinach and Broccoli with tomatoes
Spicy Cucumber and Spinach Chinese Salad
Chinese Fried Veggie Rice
Fried spicy garlic tofu with spring onions
Sweet and Sour Chinese Vegan Dish
Chinese Stir-Fry Garlic Asparagus and Mushroom
Chinese Sweet and Spicy Fried Cauliflower Florets
Creamy Chinese Ginger and Carrot soup
Vegan Chinese Spring Roll
Chinese Sweet and Spicy Seaweed Salad
Sweet Tofu Vegan Pudding
Vegan Rice Congee
One-Pot Creamy Mushroom and Green Beans Dish
Chinese Deep Fried Potato and carrot balls
Stir-Fried Garlic Pepper Pumpkin
Fried chili potatoes with green bell pepper
Mushroom with Chinese agave nectar sauce
Celery and Carrot Chinese Salad
Chinese Cabbage Noodle soup with Carrots
Mixed Mushroom Chinese Recipe

BUDDHA'S WAY

Sweet and Sour Baked Tofu
Chinese Sweet Scallion Pancake
Chili Garlic Spinach with oyster sauce
Chinese Vegan Dumpling Soup
Stir-fried Cabbage and Carrot Recipe
Stir-fried Vegetable Rice Noodles
Chinese Vegetable Salad with Fruits
Chinese Mushroom Soup
Spicy Sesame Seed Balls
Fried Baby Corns with Schezuan dipping sauce
Chinese Black Sesame Coconut Vegan Ice Cream
Fried Bananas with cinnamon and sesame seeds

INTRODUCTION

Plant based recipes were known to China ages ago through the beliefs of Buddhism and Taoism. These two beliefs focus on refraining from consumption of animals and animal products, thus resulting to the creation of vegetarian recipes. Throughout time, simple vegan recipes evolved into refined dishes that restaurants offer to its native locals and even tourists visiting China.

Vegetables become a major part in dishes offered by Chinese restaurants and are considered the most important food in China second to rice.

There are numerous restaurants all over China, which serve vegetable dishes in simple to complex, and traditional to modern recipes. This cookbook contains easy vegetable recipes and elaborate dishes that are commonly seen in traditional restaurants and even modern restaurants in China. Recipes in this cookbook promote health through nutritious facts on eating different types of vegetables.

Spicy Stir-Fried Eggplant with Snap Beans

Ingredients:

- 3 cups eggplant (cut into 2 inch long)
- 2 cups snap beans (cut into 2 inch long)
- 4 cloves garlic (minced)
- 2 tsp. of ginger (cut into thin strips)
- 1/4 cup green onions (chopped)
- 1 tsp fine black pepper
- 5 dried chili peppers (chopped)
- 1 red bell pepper (cut into small pieces)
- 1/4 cup vegetable oil
- 2 1/2 cup of water
- 4 tbsp. light soy sauce (lee kum kee)
- 2 tbsp. oyster sauce (lee kum kee)
- 1 tsp chili garlic sauce (lee kum kee)
- Small amount of salt

Utensils Needed:

- Wok (for stir fry)
- Sauce pan (for cooking the snap beans)
- Bamboo strainer
- Wok spatula
- Cutting board
- Cleaver

Directions:

Prepare all the necessary ingredients and utensils needed. Wash all the vegetables with water. Using the cleaver cut the eggplants into the cutting board for about 2 inches long. Slit the tendon of the snap beans then cut into 2 inches long using the cleaver. Sliced the red bell pepper and removed the seeds then cut into small pieces. Chopped the dried chili pepper and green onions. Remove the skin of the ginger and cut into thin strips.

Peel the covering of the garlic clove then minced.

Preheat a wok, and then pour 2 tbsp. of vegetable oil over a medium heat. Add 3 cups of eggplant (cut into 2 inches long). Fry for about 3-4 minutes until slightly brown. Remove the eggplants using a bamboo strainer and put in a bowl then set aside. Now fill a saucepan with 2 1/2 cups of water, wait until water boils then add 2 cups of snap beans (cut into 2 inches long). Heat for about 2-3 minutes over a medium heat until beans turned to yellowish green. Remove the snap beans using a bamboo streamer then rinse with cold water. Put it in a bowl then set aside.

Using the same oil from frying the eggplant, add 4 cloves of garlic (minced), ¼-cup green onions (chopped) and 5 dried chili peppers (chopped) over a medium heat. Stir-fry for about 5-7 seconds, and then add 2 slices of ginger (cut into thin strips) and 1 bell pepper (cut into small pieces). Toss and stir-fry until all ingredients are mix well. Pour 4 tbsp. of oyster sauce, 2 tbsp. of light sauce, 1 tsp chili garlic sauce and 1 tsp fine black pepper into the wok, mix well with other ingredients. Now, you can add the cooked eggplant and snap beans into the wok and stir-fry for about 3-4 minutes. Further, add small amount of salt to taste. Put in a plate and serve hot. You can now enjoy the spicy stir-fried eggplant with snap beans. Serves six people.

Health Tips:

- Eggplant contains polyphenols that aids in fighting cancer cells. It inhibits cancer growth and guard cells from free radicals. Having eggplant as main ingredient in recipes keep our cells healthy and strong.
- Dried chili pepper has a substance called capsaicin, which is responsible for the power-

ful taste that chili adds to recipes. Capsaicin produces heat sensation once in contact with mucous membrane that assists in clearing discharges from clogged nose, so make sure to add some chili pepper in dishes when experiencing colds, it surely is a congestion relief.

Steamed Baby Bok Choy with Shiitake Mushroom sauce

Ingredients:

- 350 grams' fresh baby Bok Choy
- 5 pieces large fresh Shiitake mushroom (julienned)
- 3 small cloves garlic (grated)
- 7-8 grams' ginger (thin strips)
- 1 tbsp. vegetable oil
- 1 tsp. cornstarch
- 3 tbsp. water for stir fry and another 2 cups water for steaming
- 1 tsp sesame oil
- 1 tbsp. oyster sauce (lee kum kee)
- 2 tbsp. light soy sauce (lee kum kee)
- 1 tsp. of sugar
- fine black pepper to taste
- Salt to taste

Utensils Needed:

- Wok (for cooking the mushroom sauce)
- Wok Hoak
- Bamboo Strainer (for steaming baby Bok Choy)
- Cleaver (cutting vegetable)
- Cutting Board

Directions:

Wash the ¾ pounds of baby Bok Choy with cold water thoroughly. Cut the base of the baby Bok Choy then separate each leaf. Discard any yellow or dried leaves. Prepare 5 pieces of large and fresh Shiitake mushroom. Wash it with water then cut the stems of the mushroom, leaving the mushroom caps. Chopped it into thin strips using the cleaver. Grate the garlic and cut the red ginger into thin strips.

Steam the baby Bok Choy using the bamboo streamer. Pour 2 cups of water into the wok. Placed the bamboo strainer over the wok. Put the baby Bok Choy in the strainer. Turn stove on high heat. Do not let the water touch the strainer. Steam until Bok Choy stalks turn translucent. Place the baby Bok Choy in a plate, and then set aside. Discard the water from the wok then heat the wok over medium flame. Put 1 tbsp. of vegetable oil and then add garlic. Sautee until light brown. Put in the Shiitake mushrooms and stir-fry for 1-2 minutes. Pour 3 tbsp. of water into the wok, and then combine the light soy sauce, oyster sauce, sesame oil and sugar. Mix well and let it simmer. Thicken the sauce with cornstarch and cook for 4-5 minutes. Add pepper and salt to taste. Pour the sauce using wok hoak over the cooked baby Bok Choy. Serve with thin strips of ginger on top. Serves six people.

Health Tips:

- Shiitake mushroom helps reduce blood cholesterol level in the body. It has a compound called Eritadenine and B-glucan which lowers fat level in the body, and can also keep you feeling satisfied. If you want to avoid unwanted flab, then eat some shiitake mushroom.

Stir-fried Broccoli with Sesame Garlic Sauce

Ingredients:

- 450 grams of Broccoli (remove stalks)
- 1 tbsp. garlic (crushed)
- 1 tbsp. sesame oil
- 1 tbsp. sesame seeds
- ¼ cup vegetable stock
- 1 ½ tbsp. oyster sauce
- 2 tsp vegetable oil

Utensils Needed:

- Wok (for stir0fry)
- Wok spatula
- Cleaver
- Cutting Board
- Mixing bowl

Directions:

Prepare the 450 grams' broccoli and removed the stalks. Cut it into small size broccoli florets and rinsed with water, then set aside. Remove the husk of 2 cloves garlic (1 tbsp.) and crushed with cleaver. Combine ½ cup of vegetable stock, 1 tbsp. of sesame oil, 1 ½ tbsp. of oyster sauce, and crushed ginger thoroughly in a bowl.

Put the wok on the stove and heat over medium flame. Pour in 2 tsp. of vegetable oil to the wok and add the small broccoli florets. Stir-fry for about 2 minutes. Now, put 1 tbsp. of sesame seeds and stir-fry for another 2 minutes. Make sure the sesame seeds are evenly cooked. Continuously stir the ingredients until mixed. Get the prepared garlic sauce and pour into the wok. Let it simmer then reduce the heat. Wait for another 2-3 minutes until cook. Be careful not to overdo the broccoli. Serves 4 person.

Health Tips:

- It is extensively researched that Broccoli fights cancer in different ways. It increases the fighting capacity of human immune system. It enhances the digestive system. It decreases the blood cholesterol level in the body and reduces inflammation. It is also a very good source of vitamin C and a powerful antioxidant. Many recipes should have broccoli in them. An amazing vegetable that prevents cancer so well.

Sesame Ginger Noodles with Steamed Tofu and Broccoli

Ingredients:

- 300 grams rice noodles
- 250 grams tofu (cut into small square blocks)
- 250 grams broccoli florets
- 3 tbsp. ginger (cut into thin strips)
- 3 tbsp. sesame seeds
- 1 large dried chili (chopped)
- 3 small cloves of garlic (minced)
- 2 scallions (chopped)
- 1 tsp. sesame oil
- 1 tsp. vegetable oil
- 2 tbsp. light soy sauce
- ¼ cup vegetable stock
- 4 cups water
- 2 tsp. cornstarch
- 1 tsp. brown sugar

Utensils Needed:

- Wok (for combining all ingredients)
- Large pot (for cooking noodles)
- Steamer (for steaming broccoli and tofu)
- Colander (for straining noodles)
- Wok chuan (spatula)
- Cleaver
- Cutting board

Directions:

Turn on the stove to high heat and boil 4 cups of water in a large pot. Once water boils, turn off the flame then place 300 grams of rice noodles into the pot. Let the noodles soak for about 3-4 minutes while constantly stirring every minute until you see the noodles start to separate. Do not completely cook the noodles, since you will be using it again later. Strain the noodles using a colander then set it aside.

Prepare 250 grams of broccoli florets (no stalks), rinse with water then put in a steamer for 5 minutes and save it for later use. Cut 250 grams of tofu into cubes. Steam the tofu for 5 minutes then set it aside.

Prepare all the other ingredients. Slice 2 green onions and 1 large dried chili pepper. Mince 3 cloves of garlic then cut 3 tbsp. of ginger into thin shreds.

Preheat wok over medium flame then put 1 tsp of vegetable oil. When the oil is hot, add 3 tbsp. of sesame seeds. Toast it until golden brown. Put the garlic, ginger, dried chili pepper and scallions in the wok in consecutive manner. Fry for about a minute then pour in ¼ cup of vegetable stock. Now, you can add 2 tbsp. of light soy sauce, 1 tsp of sesame oil and 1 tsp of sugar into the wok. Bring it to simmer then thicken with 2 tsp. of cornstarch. Place the cook rice noodles and combine with the sauce on low heat. Stir continuously for 2-3 minutes then turn off the heat. Mix the steamed broccoli and tofu with the noodles. Be careful when mixing with steamed tofu, it's a bit delicate. You don't want to ruin its shape. Serves 4 person.

Health Tip:

- If you want to have tougher bones, better include sesame seeds in your recipe. Sesame seed provides calcium and zinc into the body, which promotes healthy bones.

Chinese Vegan Peanut Soup

Ingredients:

- 1 cup raw peanuts (peeled and toasted)
- 5 cups water
- 1 cup cold water (for cornstarch)
- 4 cups water (for soaking peanuts)
- 2 tbsp. cornstarch
- 1/2 cup sugar
- ½ cup Bok Choy (chopped)
- ½ cup fresh spinach
- ¼ cup fresh shiitake mushroom (chopped)
- 1 tbsp. light soy sauce
- 1 tsp. Shaoxing wine (Chinese rice wine)
- Salt and pepper to taste
- Minced cilantro and crushed peanuts for garnish

Utensils Needed:

- Wok (for frying peanuts)
- Pot (for cooking the soup)
- Blender (grinding roasted peanuts)
- Wok hoak (for mixing soup)
- Cleaver
- Cutting Board
- Spatula (use for frying peanuts)
- Steamer (for steaming vegetables)

Directions:

Prepare 1 cup of peanuts. Peel and soak it in 4 cups of water overnight. Using a wok, over high heat, stir-fry the peanuts until roasted. Set it aside.

Wash vegetables with cold water. Remove the stems of the shiitake mushroom then chop the caps. Chop bok choy and spinach into small chunks. Steam each vegetable using a steamer then save for later use.

Get your roasted peanuts and put it in the blender. Mix with 1 cup of water then start grinding until smooth. It should look like a paste after blending.

Pour 1 cup of cold water into a pot and mix in 2 tbsp. of cornstarch until lumps disappear. Turn on the stove over medium flame and then add 4 cups of water and ½ cup of sugar. Put 1 tbsp. of light soy sauce and a teaspoon of Shaoxing wine. Cover the pot and let it simmer. Now, add the prepared peanut paste. Continuously stir the soup with wok hoak until smooth and thicken. Add some salt and pepper to taste. Place the steamed vegetables into the pot and mix well with the soup. Garnish with crushed peanuts and minced cilantro. Serve hot to 6 people.

Health Tip:

- Do you want to stay forever young? Peanut is the answer to the aging process. It contains Resveratrol, a strong antioxidant that is effective in slowing the course of aging.

Sweet and Sour Onion Side Dish

Ingredients:

- 500 grams small onion (peeled)
- 3 small cloves of garlic (minced)
- 1 tsp. ginger (minced)
- 1 tbsp. vegetable oil
- 2 tsp cornstarch
- 3 tbsp. cold water
- 1 tbsp. sugar
- 1 tbsp. rice vinegar
- 3 tbsp. catsup
- 1 cup water
- 1/2 tsp. salt

Utensils Needed:

- Wok
- Spatula
- Cleaver
- Cutting board
- Mixing bowl

Directions:

Rinse onion, garlic and ginger with water. Pat until dry. Peel 500 grams of small onions then mince ginger and garlic. Set aside.

In a mixing bowl, combine 3 tbsp. of cold water and 2 tsp of cornstarch until smooth. Then, pour 1 cup of water, 1 tablespoon of sugar and rice vinegar, 3 tbsp. of catsup and ½ tsp of salt. Mix all ingredients well.

Preheat wok over medium flame and put 1 tbsp. of vegetable oil. Wait until oil is hot before putting in minced garlic and a tsp of ginger. Add 500 grams of onion and sauté until translucent. Pour the sauce mixture into the wok then mix thoroughly. Cook for about

15-20 minutes while occasionally stirring. Serve soup hot to 6 people.

Health Tip:

- Peeling onions is not an easy task. Do you know that carefully peeling onions will reduce your risks of getting cancer and heart related diseases? Flavonoids, which is found mostly in the outermost layer of onions, is a phytochemical antioxidant that is responsible for prevention of cancer and cardiovascular illnesses. The next time you include onions in your recipe, be wary of peeling it cautiously.

Spicy Steamed Spinach and Bean Sprout Salad

Ingredients:

- 500 grams fresh Spinach
- 250 grams fresh Bean sprouts
- 2 tbsp. chili garlic sauce
- 1 tbsp. dark soy sauce
- 2 tsp. sesame oil
- 4 tbsp. Chinese black vinegar
- 1 tbsp. sugar
- 1 teaspoon white sesame seed

Utensils Needed:

- Steamer (for steaming vegetables)
- Large mixing bowl
- 2 wooden spoon

Directions:

Prepare 500 grams of fresh spinach and 250 grams of fresh bean sprouts. Clean with cold water. Remove any yellowish and dried spinach leaves. Take out the dark and dried tail of bean sprouts. Steam both vegetables using a steamer. Do not steam for too long.

Get a large mixing bowl. Pour 2 tbsp. of chili garlic sauce followed by 1 tbsp. of dark soy sauce, 4 tbsp. of Chinese black vinegar. Add a tablespoon of white sugar. Combine all the ingredients using a wooden spoon. Now, put two teaspoons of sesame oil and stir well. Using two wooden spoon, blend the salad dressing carefully with steamed spinach and bean sprouts. Sprinkle with a teaspoon of white sesame seed.

Health Tip:

- Do you know that the best vegetable to eat

before going to a gym is spinach? According to a study done in Stockholm, Spinach has natural nitrate components that make our muscles tougher. Due to this nitrate, production of calcium by increased levels of two important proteins found in the muscles, lead to stronger muscle contraction. Becoming fit will come easily to you when you make a dish out of Spinach or simply eat fresh spinach.

Fried Tofu with Veggies

Ingredients:

- 500 grams' tofu (cubed)
- 1 cup flat green beans (small size)
- 1 cup broccoli (florets)
- 1 large red bell pepper (sliced)
- 2 tbsp. sesame oil
- 1/3 cup light soy sauce
- 2 tablespoon oyster sauce
- 1 tablespoon ginger (grated)
- 1 tablespoon garlic (crushed)
- 1 tablespoon brown sugar
- ½ teaspoon dried chili pepper
- 1 tbsp. cornstarch
- 2 tablespoon of cold water

Utensils Needed:

- Wok
- Spatula
- Cleaver
- Cutting board
- Mixing bowl

Directions:

Prepare all the ingredients. Wash vegetables with cold running water, and then pat to dry. Cut the stalks of broccoli, leaving the florets. Slit the tendons of the flat green beans. Slice 1 large red bell pepper and remove the seeds. Carefully cut 500 grams of tofu using a cleaver and a cutting board into small cubes. Grate 1 tablespoon of ginger and mince 1 tablespoon of garlic, set them aside.

In a mixing bowl, put 1/3 cup of light soy sauce, mix it with 2 tablespoons of oyster sauce. Put a tablespoon of brown sugar and ½ a teaspoon of dried chili pepper. Mix a tablespoon of cornstarch and 2 tablespoons of cold water then pour into the mixing bowl. Combine the liquid mixture well and save it for later use.

Place wok over medium flame. Pour 2 tablespoon of sesame oil into the wok and wait until hot before putting garlic. Put the ginger when the garlic turn to slightly brown. When you can smell the aroma of garlic and ginger, mix in the tofu and stir-fry until golden. Get the prepared liquid mixture and pour into the wok. Let it simmer. Now, place broccoli and flat green beans into the wok and stir-fry for about 4-5 minutes. Add the slice red bell pepper and make sure to stir thoroughly all the ingredients. Cook for additional 2-3 minutes. Serves 6 person.

Health Tips:

- Do you want a healthy glowing skin and a strong body to fight off infection? A cup of red bell pepper contains a lot of vitamin C compared to an orange. This means eating red bell pepper will give your immune system a higher protection against virus and bacteria. It will also keep your skin healthy, and your bones and teeth stronger.

Steamed Wonton Veggies

Ingredients:

- 40-45 wonton wrapper
- ½ cup carrots (grated)
- ½ cup potatoes (grated)
- ½ cup spinach (coarsely chopped)
- ¼ cup mushroom (finely chopped)
- 2 tbsp. of red bell pepper (minced)
- 2 tbsp. of scallions (minced)
- 2 tsp. ginger (grated)
- 2 tablespoon soy sauce
- 1 tablespoon hoisin sauce
- 2 tsp. sesame oil
- 1 teaspoon salt
- ½ teaspoon fine black pepper
- Water for boiling

<u>Dipping sauce:</u>

- 60 ml soy sauce
- 2 tsp grated ginger
- 60ml vinegar
- 2 tsp hot sauce
- 2 tsp minced garlic

Utensils Needed:

- Bamboo Steamer
- Cleaver
- Cutting Board
- Large mixing bowl
- Vegetable Shredder
- 2 sauce bowl

Directions:

Rinse all vegetable with cold running water and pat to dry. Get a cleaver and cutting board, then coarsely chop a ½ cup of spinach. Cut the mushroom into small pieces. Mince 2 tablespoons of scallions and red bell pepper. Using a shredder, grate carrots, potatoes and ginger. Save all ingredients for later use.

In a large mixing bowl, pour in 2 tablespoons of soy sauce, 1 tablespoon of hoisin sauce and 2 teaspoon of sesame oil. Add a teaspoon of salt and ½ a teaspoon of fine black pepper. Combine liquid ingredients well. Put all the vegetable ingredients into the bowl and mix thoroughly. Set it aside.

Get your wonton wrapper. Place a teaspoon of vegetable mixture into the center of the wrapper. Wet all the edges of the wrapper with water and then fold into desired shape. Repeat procedure until all the wrappers are used.

Boil ½ inch of water using a steamer over medium flame. Place each wonton dumplings in a single layer on the steamer. Be careful not to let wonton touch each other. Steam for about 10-12 minutes and repeat procedure until all the dumplings are cooked.

For the dipping sauce. Combine 60 ml of soy sauce and ½ a teaspoon of grated ginger. For another sauce, mix 60 ml of vinegar, ½ teaspoon of hot sauce and ½ teaspoon of minced garlic into a sauce bowl.

Health Tip:
- Potatoes has dropping substance for blood pressure called kukoamines. It also contains more potassium than bananas that helps lower blood pressure. Moreover, fiber in potatoes help reduce blood cholesterol level in the body that aids in lowering blood pressure as well.

Stir fry Spinach and Broccoli with tomatoes

Ingredients:

- 2 cups of spinach (chopped)
- 2 cups of broccoli (chopped)
- 1 cup of tomatoes (sliced)
- 1 large onion (sliced)
- 1 garlic clove (minced)
- 2 tablespoon olive oil
- 2 tablespoon soy sauce
- 1 teaspoon rice vinegar
- 1 teaspoon salt
- ½ teaspoon fine black pepper

Utensils Needed:

- Wok
- Spatula
- Cutting board
- Cleaver

Directions:

Get your cleaver and cutting board. Wash onion and garlic with water and pat to dry. Julienne 1 large onion and mince the garlic. Cut the broccoli stem and discard, leaving the head, chop into small pieces. Chop 2 cups of spinach and 1 cup of tomatoes. Set aside the vegetables.

Put 2 tablespoon of olive oil in a wok, over medium heat. Wait until oil is hot before adding the garlic and onion. Sauté until garlic is slightly brown and onion is translucent. Pour in 2 tablespoons of soy sauce and 1 teaspoon of rice vinegar into the wok. Stir for a minute. Add the broccoli and stir-fry for 2-3 minutes. Put the spinach and tomatoes and mix well with the other ingredients.

Do not overcook the vegetables. Season with 1 teaspoon of salt and ½ a teaspoon of fine black pepper. Let it cook for another minute while stirring frequently. Serves 4-5 person.

Health Tip:

- If you want your eyes to stay healthy, you should eat more tomatoes. Tomatoes are highly pigmented vegetable. This pigmented substance is called carotenoids. It includes lycopene, beta-carotene and lutein. Per various studies, these substances help in preventing eye related problems. Tomatoes also contains vitamin A, C and E, which are responsible for, maintain a good eyesight.

Spicy Cucumber and Spinach Chinese Salad

Ingredients:

- 2 large Cucumbers (thin-skinned)
- 450 grams Spinach (chopped)
- 1 large tomato (sliced)
- 1 medium size Onion (sliced)
- 1/3 cup rice vinegar
- 1 tablespoon light soy sauce
- 1 teaspoon sugar
- 1/2 teaspoon dried chili pepper
- ½ teaspoon fine black pepper
- 2 teaspoon sesame oil
- 1 teaspoon chili garlic sauce
- ½ teaspoon salt

Utensils Needed:

- Large mixing bowl
- 2 wooden spoon
- Cleaver
- Cutting board

Directions:

Wash all the vegetables with water. Get your cleaver and cutting board. Coarsely chop 450 grams of spinach and set aside. Peel the cucumber skin thinly and thinly slice the cucumbers. Do the same with onion and tomatoes, cutting it thinly and save for later use.

In a large mixing bowl, mix first all liquid ingredients. Start with 1/3 cup of rice vinegar, followed by 1 tablespoon of light soy sauce, and then add 1 teaspoon of chili garlic sauce. Now add 2 teaspoons of sesame oil and whisk thoroughly. Put ½ teaspoon of dried chili pepper, ½ teaspoon of fine black pepper and ½ teaspoon of salt.

Mix well. Lastly, add 1 teaspoon of sugar in the liquid mixture and combine well.

Get your prepared vegetables and toss it using two wooden spoon with the salad mixture. Serves 3-4 person as side dish. Serves 1-2 person as main salad dish.

Health Tip:

- Did you know that you could eat water? Cucumber has the highest amount of water among many vegetables and fruits. So, it feels like you are eating water when you have cucumbers as food. It's perfect for salad or you can just plainly eat it specially during summer and you won't feel thirsty at all.

Chinese Fried Veggie Rice

Ingredients:

- 3 cups cooked rice
- ¼ cup green beans (finely chopped)
- ¼ cup white onion ((chopped) and 2 tablespoon green onions for garnish
- ¼ cup shiitake mushroom (sliced into small pieces)
- ¼ cup carrots (finely chopped)
- ¼ cup green peas
- ¼ cup cabbage (finely chopped)
- ¼ cup green bell pepper (finely chopped)
- 2 teaspoon celery (finely chopped)
- 4 small clove garlic (minced)
- 2 tablespoon soy sauce
- 2 teaspoon rice vinegar
- 2 tablespoon vegetable oil
- 1 teaspoon salt
- 1 teaspoon fine black pepper

Utensils Needed:

- Wok
- Spatula
- Cutting board
- Cleaver

Directions:

Prepare all your vegetables. Wash with cold water and pat to dry. Using your cleaver and cutting board, finely chopped all the vegetables (carrots, shiitake mushroom, green bell pepper, cabbage, white onion, green beans and celery). Peel 4 small cloves of garlic and mince. Set aside for later use.

Prepare your cooked rice and make sure the rice is cool enough before putting it in a wok for frying. If you are using left over rice, break rice individually to avoid clumped rice.

In a wok over high heat, put in 2 tablespoons of vegetable oil. When the oil is hot, add the garlic and sauté. When you can smell the aroma of the garlic, you can now add green beans and green peas. Stir-fry for about 2-3 minutes. You should always cook these vegetables first since they take longer to cook. Put the carrots, cabbage, mushroom, celery and green bell pepper thereafter. Add 1 cup of rice one at a time and mix well with the vegetables until you finish adding all 3 cups of rice. Continuously toss the vegetables and rice until cooked evenly. Pour the soy sauce and vinegar into the fried rice and frequently stir so that sauce will combine well with the rice and vegetables. Season with salt and pepper. Put in a large plate and garnish with green onions. Serves 2-3 persons.

Health Tip:

- Having problems with digestion? Simply eat some green peas and you will have a healthy tummy. Green peas contains high amount of fiber that is helpful in digestion. You won't have any problems with constipation as well, since the fiber content in green peas aids in peristalsis.

Fried spicy garlic tofu with spring onions

Ingredients:

- 350 grams tofu (cubed)
- 1 teaspoon of spring onions
- 2 large cloves garlic (minced)
- 1 teaspoon red dried chili pepper (finely chopped)
- 4 tablespoon soy sauce
- 2 teaspoon cornstarch
- 2 tablespoon cold water
- 1 tablespoon vegetable oil
- 1/2 teaspoon white sesame seeds
- Salt and pepper to taste

Utensils Needed:

- Wok
- Spatula
- Cutting board
- Cleaver
- Mixing Bowl

Directions:

Dice your tofu and set it aside. Wash and peel your garlic and mince it. Finely chop dried chili pepper and spring onions and save for later use.

In a mixing bowl, combine 2 tablespoons of cold water and 2 teaspoons of cornstarch. Mix until there are no more clumps. Now, add 4 tablespoons of soy sauce and 1 teaspoon of dried chili pepper. Whisk thoroughly then set aside.

Over medium flame, heat 2 tablespoons of vegetable oil and add garlic once oil is hot. Wait until garlic is slightly golden before adding the cubed tofu. Stir-fry for 3-4 minutes and then season with salt and pepper.

Pour the liquid mixture into the wok and stir-fry for another 3-4 minutes until tofu is crispy. Once cook, place on a plate, garnish with spring onions and white sesame seeds. Serve hot to 4-5 persons.

Health Tip:

- Are you suffering from common cold? Make sure to have spring onions readily available in your kitchen. Spring onions has anti-viral compounds that treats common cold. It has always been used to treat respiratory problems since ancient times.

Sweet and Sour Chinese Vegan Dish

Ingredients:

- ½ cup flat green beans (trimmed)
- ½ cup cauliflower florets (sliced)
- ½ cup bean sprouts
- ½ cup baby corn cubs
- ½ cup pineapple chunks
- ½ cup tomatoes (crushed)
- ¼ cup red bell pepper (chopped)
- ¼ cup green bell pepper (chopped)
- ¼ cup yellow bell pepper (chopped)
- ¼ cup onions (sliced)
- 1/2 cup cold water
- 2 teaspoon cornstarch
- 1 tablespoon soy sauce
- 1 tablespoon rice vinegar
- 1 teaspoon sugar
- 2 teaspoon vegetable oil
- Salt to taste

Utensils Needed:

- Wok
- Spatula
- Cutting board
- Cleaver
- Large Mixing bowl

Directions:

Prepare all your vegetables. Wash them with cold running water. Trim the tendon of flat green beans. Cut the dark tail end of bean sprouts. Slice cauliflower florets into small sizes. Chop green, yellow and red bell pepper into small pieces. You can cut the baby corn cubs into half or leave it as whole. Slice onions and tomatoes. Set all the vegetables aside for later use.

Get a large mixing bowl and whisk ½ cup of cold water and 2 teaspoons of cornstarch. When the cornstarch mixture has no more clumps, add a tablespoon of soy sauce and rice vinegar. Mix thoroughly. Now add a teaspoon of sugar and put the slice tomatoes. Crush the tomatoes well and combine with the liquid mixture.

In a wok, over medium flame, put 2 teaspoons of vegetable oil. Once oil is hot enough, put the sliced onions and wait until it becomes translucent before adding the vegetables. Put the flat green beans first because it takes long to cook. Stir for about 1-2 minutes, then add all the other vegetables, while continuously tossing each vegetable in the wok. Put the pineapple into the wok after adding all the vegetables. Cook for about 3-4 minutes before adding the sweet and sour sauce. Do not overcook the vegetables. Coat the vegetables well with the sauce by stirring frequently. Season with salt and mix well. Serves 4 persons.

Health tip:

- Pineapple might look weird because of its spikes and shape but this fruit contains high amount of copper, which helps in blood circulation. Copper is one of the responsible compound that makes red blood cells. Red blood cells carry oxygen throughout the body that makes cells live, keeping different organs healthy.

Chinese Stir-Fry Garlic Asparagus and Mushroom

Ingredients:

- 350 grams asparagus
- 200 grams shiitake mushrooms
- 1 large garlic clove (minced)
- 3 tablespoon soy sauce
- 1 tablespoon vegetable oil
- 1 teaspoon chili garlic sauce
- 1 teaspoon sesame seeds
- Salt and pepper to taste

Utensils Needed:

- Wok
- Spatula
- Cutting board
- Cleaver

Directions:

Wash asparagus and shiitake mushrooms with cold running water. Cut the asparagus into 2-inch size. Slice mushroom into medium size. Peel the garlic and mince. Set aside.

Pour a tablespoon of vegetable oil into a wok over medium heat. When the oil is hot, add the garlic. Put the asparagus and stir-fry with a spatula until tender then add the shiitake and stir continuously for about 2-3 minutes. Pour 3 tablespoon of soy sauce and a teaspoon of chili garlic sauce then mix with the vegetables until well coated. Season with sesame seeds, salt and pepper. Cook for another 1-2 minutes then serve hot to 4 persons.

Health Tip:

- Garlic is well known for treating and preventing cardiovascular disease. It contains anti-inflammatory substance that prevents plaque formation into the blood vessels specially vessels of the heart. Just adding garlic in your dish, will make your heart healthy.

Chinese Sweet and Spicy Fried Cauliflower Florets

Ingredients:

- 1 head cauliflower (cut into small florets)
- 2 medium size tomatoes (sliced)
- 1 green bell pepper (diced)
- 4 cloves garlic (minced)
- 1 inch ginger (peeled and julienned)
- 2 tablespoon green onions (chopped)
- 1 tablespoon vegetable oil
- 3 tablespoon light soy sauce
- ½ cup vegetable broth
- ¼ cup cold water
- 2 tablespoon cornstarch
- 1 teaspoon hoisin sauce
- 2 teaspoon dried chili pepper
- 1 teaspoon sugar
- 1 teaspoon agave nectar
- Salt and pepper to taste

Utensils Needed:

- Wok
- Spatula
- Cutting board
- Cleaver
- Large mixing bowl

Directions:

Rinse vegetables with cold water. Cut the cauliflower into small florets using your cleaver. Sliced two medium size tomatoes and chop 1 green bell pepper. Set them aside. Peel 4 cloves of garlic and mince. Peel 1 inch ginger and cut into thin strips. Cut green scallions into small pieces and save for later use.

Combine liquid mixture in a mixing bowl. Put first ¼ cup of cold water and mix with 2 tablespoons of cornstarch. Then add 3 tablespoons of light soy sauce and 1 teaspoon of hoisin sauce. Put 2 teaspoon of dried chili pepper and a teaspoon of agave nectar and sugar. You can now put the slice tomatoes and crush it in the mixture. Mix well. Set the sauce aside.

Over medium flame, put 1 tablespoon of vegetable oil into a wok. Wait until oil is hot before putting the garlic. Add the cauliflower florets and stir-fry for about 4-5 minutes until slightly brown. Mix in the green bell pepper and scallions and continue stirring for about a minute, then add ½ cup of vegetable broth. Let it simmer before pouring in the sweet and spicy sauce. Toss the vegetables into the sauce thoroughly and then bring it to boil. Season with salt and pepper. Cook for another minute then serve hot to 4 persons.

Health Tip:

- Cauliflower contains B Vitamin Choline, which is responsible for keeping human brain cells healthy. If you don't want to experience frequent memory gaps, then include cauliflower in your recipes.

Creamy Chinese Ginger and Carrot soup

Ingredients:

- 500 grams carrots (peeled and cubed)
- 3 tablespoon ginger (peeled and grated)
- 6 cups vegetable broth
- 1 cup coconut milk
- 1 onion (minced)
- 2 tablespoon vegetable oil
- 1 teaspoon fine black pepper
- Salt to taste
- Cilantro for garnish

Utensils needed:

- Large pot
- Blender
- Cleaver
- Cutting board
- Shredder
- Peeler

Directions:

Wash carrots and peel the skin. Cut into cubes. Rinse the ginger and peel the skin, and then using a shredder, grate 3 tablespoons of ginger. Skin the onion and mince, then set aside.

In a large pot, over medium flame, heat 2 tablespoons of vegetable oil. Put onion then sauté until translucent. Add 500 grams of cubed carrots and 3 tablespoons of grated ginger. Stir-fry 2-3 minutes. Pour 6 cups of vegetable broth and let it boil. Cook until carrots are tender. Remove the flame and prepare your blender.

Put the carrot mixture in a blender and combine 1 cup of coconut milk. Blend until creamy. Turn on your stove and put a large pot over medium heat. Pour your mixture into the pot and let it simmer. Season with 1 teaspoon of black pepper and salt. Serve hot to 4 persons.

Health Tip:

- Cilantro is best as a detoxifying agent for metals like lead, aluminum and arsenic. Our body sometimes accumulate these metals in very small amount and allowing them to stay in the body in large amount is harmful. Eating cilantro helps in removing this toxic waste.

Vegan Chinese Spring Roll

Ingredients:

- 1 cup cabbage (shredded)
- 10 shiitake mushroom (finely chopped)
- 2 carrots (grated)
- 2 potatoes (grated)
- 1 cup bean sprouts
- 50 spring roll wrappers
- 1 tablespoon cornstarch
- 3 tablespoon cold water
- 1 stalk scallion (finely chopped)
- 1 tablespoon vegetable oil plus 4 tablespoon vegetable oil for frying
- 2 tablespoon light soy sauce
- 1 tablespoon Shaoxing wine
- 3 cloves garlic (minced)
- Pepper to taste
- Soy sauce or ketchup (dipping sauce)

Utensils Needed:

- Wok
- Spatula
- Cutting board
- Cleaver
- Shredder
- Small mixing bowl

Directions:

Prepare your vegetables. Rinse with cold water and pat to dry. Peel carrots, garlic and potatoes. Grate potatoes, cabbage and carrots using a shredder. Cut garlic into extremely small pieces. Finely cup scallions and shiitake mushroom. Remove the dark or dried tail end of bean sprouts. Set all the vegetables aside for stir-frying.

In a wok, put 1 tablespoon of vegetable oil over

medium flame. Add garlic and wait until it turns slightly brown. Combine all the vegetables in the wok, start with potatoes and carrots, followed by mushrooms, bean sprouts, cabbage and scallions. Stir-fry for about 2-3 minutes. Pour the soy sauce and Shaoxing wine into the wok and stir-fry for another 2 minutes until all the vegetables are coated well. Season with pepper.

In a small mixing bowl, put 3 tablespoons of cold water and 1 tablespoon of cornstarch until no more clumps can be seen. Prepare your spring roll wrappers. Wet all the edges of the wrapper with cornstarch mixture. Place a tablespoon of vegetables on the corner of the wrapper and then roll the edge tightly over the vegetable mixture. Cover each side tightly while wrapping add more cornstarch mixture on each side to secure. Once at the other edge of the wrapper, secure it with cornstarch liquid mixture.

In a wok, over high heat, put 4 tablespoons of vegetable oil. Wait until oil is hot before placing spring rolls. Fry each side of the spring roll and cook until golden.

You can use soy sauce or ketchup for dipping sauce.

Health Tip:

- Cabbage contains less calories compared to other vegetables, which means eating a lot of it won't make you fat. You don't have to worry in keeping your body slim when you're eating a bunch of cabbage.

Chinese Sweet and Spicy Seaweed Salad

Ingredients:

- 250 grams wet seaweed (julienned)
- 2 small carrots (julienned)
- 2 tablespoon light soy sauce
- 2 teaspoon Chinese black vinegar
- 2 teaspoon sugar
- 2 teaspoon chili pepper (powder)
- ¼ cup parsley (chopped)
- 2 tablespoon olive oil
- 2 teaspoon sesame seeds
- 1 bunch of spring onion (chopped)
- Salt and pepper to taste

Utensils Needed:

- Large mixing bowl
- Two wooden spoon
- Cleaver
- Cutting board
- Pot
- Bamboo strainer

Directions:

Clean your seaweed with cold water and cut into thin strips. Boil water in a pot, then cook seaweed for about 1 minute. Using a bamboo strainer, remove seaweed from the pot and rinse with cold water. Set aside.

Peel 2 carrots and cut into thin strips. Wash parsley and spring onion then chop. Save for later use.

Get a large mixing bowl and combine all liquid ingredients first. Pour 2 tablespoon of light soy sauce, 2 tablespoons of olive oil, and 2 teaspoons of black vinegar. Stir well using a wooden spoon. Add 2 teaspoon of sugar,

2 teaspoons of chili pepper and 2 teaspoons of sesame seeds. Make sure to mix thoroughly all the ingredients. Now, add your seaweed, carrots, parsley and spring onion. Toss using two wooden spoon until all vegetables are coated well. Sprinkle with a pinch of salt and pepper. Serve cold to 2-3 persons.

Health Tip:

- Seaweed is rich source of Iodine. Eating seaweed will keep you from getting thyroid problems, thus keeping hormones in the body balanced and regulated well.

Sweet Tofu Vegan Pudding

Ingredients:

- 3 cups unsweetened soy milk
- 1 teaspoon potato starch
- 1 teaspoon gypsum or you can also use Epsom salt
- 2 pcs 1 inch ginger (grated)
- ½ cup brown sugar
- 1 cup water (for ginger syrup) and 2 tablespoon + 2 teaspoon water (for gypsum)
- Parsley or cilantro for garnish

Utensils Needed:

- Pot
- Saucepan
- Wooden spatula
- Hoak or ladle
- Shredder
- Mixing bowl
- Small bowl

Directions:

Get a mixing bowl and combine a teaspoon of potato starch and gypsum. If you want grainy type of tofu pudding, you can use Epsom salt. Add 2 tablespoon + 2 teaspoon of water. Mix well.

In a saucepan, put 2 cups of unsweetened soymilk and let it boil. Remove foam. Now, get a pot preferably large pot, for settling the soymilk when it turns jelly like. Put the gypsum and starch mixture first into the large pot then pour the soymilk 1 foot above the pot. This will ensure that soymilk and gypsum are evenly mix. Cover with a cloth and let it set for an hour until tofu becomes jelly like in appearance.

Peel 2 pcs of 1 inch ginger and grate using a shredder. Put in a saucepan together with 1 cup of water, ½ cup of brown sugar. Over low heat, stir using wooden spatula until syrup thickens.

Using a hoak, put some tofu pudding in a small bowl, and then pour some ginger syrup. Garnish with parsley or cilantro. Serves hot or cold to 3 people.

Health tip:

- Gypsum is a good source of calcium. For women who don't want to suffer from bone diseases when they get old, adding gypsum in some dishes would help them increase calcium intake thus preventing illnesses of the bone.

Vegan Rice Congee

Ingredients:

- 1 cup rice (jasmine rice)
- 4 cups water
- 150 grams pumpkin (grated)
- 150 grams potato (grated)
- ¼ cup mushroom (cut into small pieces)
- 50 grams carrots (grated)
- 4 cups vegetable broth
- 1 tablespoon ginger (minced)
- 1 tablespoon garlic (minced)
- 1 tablespoon white onion (minced)
- 1 tablespoon light soy sauce
- Salt to taste
- Red pepper flakes, powdered black pepper and chopped spring onion (for garnish)

Utensils Needed:

- Large Pot
- Ladle or hoak
- Shredder
- Blender
- Cleaver
- Cutting board
- Steamer

Directions:

Clean all vegetables and peel carrots, pumpkin and potatoes. Wash mushroom with cold running water and remove the stem. Get a steamer and steam all vegetables until tender. Cut the mushroom into small pieces and set aside. Shred potatoes, carrots and pumpkin and put in a blender. Blend until thicken. Save for later use.

Wash rice with water before cooking. In a large pot, pour 4 cups of water and 4 cups of vegetable broth.

Put into the pot 1 tablespoon of minced garlic, onion and ginger. Pour 1 tablespoon of light soy sauce and let it simmer. Now, add 1 cup of rice. Cook until rice grain can easily be broken. If you want lighter consistency of rice porridge, you can add more water or vegetable broth. Combine the blended vegetables and mushroom, then season with salt. Mix everything well using a ladle. Cover the pot and bring it to boil.

Serve hot to 7-8 persons. Garnish with red pepper flakes, powdered black pepper and chopped spring onions.

Health Tip:

- Do you want to get enough sleep and feel happy all the time? Make sure to add some pumpkin in your daily meal. It contains tryptophan that improves sleep pattern and aids in increasing serotonin level in the body, one of the main neurotransmitter in the body that makes people joyful.

One-Pot Creamy Mushroom and Green Beans Dish

Ingredients:

- 500 grams mushroom (diced)
- 500 grams green beans (cut into 2 inches long)
- 1 cup coconut milk
- ½ cup vegetable broth
- 1 tablespoon onion (minced)
- 1 tablespoon garlic (minced)
- 1 tablespoon light soy sauce
- 1 teaspoon Shaoxing wine
- 2 tablespoon cold water
- 2 teaspoon cornstarch
- 2 tablespoon vegetable oil
- Salt and pepper to taste
- Parsley (coarsely chopped for garnish)

Utensils Needed:

- Pot
- Cleaver
- Cutting board
- Small mixing bowl

Directions:

Clean your mushroom and green beans. Cut the stem of the mushroom leaving the cap behind. Dice the mushroom cap. Trim the green beans and cut into 2-inch long. Clean the onions and garlic with cold water and mince. Set aside.

In a mixing bowl, combine 2 teaspoons of cornstarch and 2 tablespoons of cold water. Save for later use.

Put 2 tablespoon of oil into a pot. Wait until oil is shimmering before adding onions and garlic. Coat onions and garlic with oil by stirring continuously. Add the green beans and sit-fry for 2-3 minutes, and then put the mushroom next. Continue stirring to cook the vegetables evenly. Pour 1 cup of milk and ½ cup of vegetable broth into the pot. Cover and let it boil. Now, mix in the soy sauce and Shaoxing wine. Season with salt and pepper and bring to simmer. Add the cornstarch mixture and wait until dish thickens. Stir occasionally and do not overcook the vegetables. Serve hot to 4-5 persons.

Health Tip:

- Joint pain is common to elderly people but even the younger generation is experiencing this kind of pain due to poor body movements and improper posture. If you want to avoid this kind of pain, add parsley into your meal. This herb acts as anti-inflammatory agent, which prevents joint pain.

Chinese Deep Fried Potato and carrot balls

Ingredients:

- 500 grams potatoes (steamed and mashed)
- 250 grams carrots (steamed and mashed)
- 1 and ½ cup glutinous rice flour
- 3 tablespoon all-purpose flour
- ½ cup water
- 2 tablespoon vinegar
- 2 teaspoon baking soda
- 1 teaspoon salt
- 1 teaspoon powdered black pepper
- 1 teaspoon cilantro
- 1 teaspoon garlic
- 2 cups of vegetable oil

Utensils Needed:

- Pot
- Strainer
- Deep frying pan
- Cutting board
- Cleaver
- Wooden fork
- Mixing bowl

Directions:

Clean and peel potatoes and carrots. Place in a pot of boiling water. Cook until carrots and potatoes are tender. Drain using a colander. Let it cool then pat to dry. Cut into cubes and then mash in a bowl using a wooden fork. Mix in minced cilantro, salt, pepper and garlic. Combine all ingredients thoroughly. Set aside.

In a separate bowl, put 1 and ½ cup of sticky rice flour and 3 tablespoons of all-purpose flour. Mix well and then add ½ cup of water.

Get a small mixing bowl and combine 2 tablespoons of vinegar and 2 teaspoons of baking soda. Whisk until foamy.

Now, get your potato and carrot mixture, combine with the rice flour mixture and baking soda-vinegar mixture. Knead the dough until all ingredients are mixed. Shape a tablespoon of the mixture into a ball. Repeat procedure until all the mixture are used.

In a deep-frying pan, over high heat. Put 2 cups of vegetable oil. Wait until oil is shimmering before putting in the potato-carrot balls. Deep fry for 3 minutes or until golden brown. Serve 25-30 potato-carrot balls. You can use ketchup for dipping sauce.

Health Tip:

- Carrots is rich source of beta-carotene, which promotes good eyesight. Per studies, higher intake of beta-carotene prevents elderly from acquiring macular degeneration, an eye disease causing vision loss.

Stir-Fried Garlic Pepper Pumpkin

Ingredients:

- 500 grams pumpkin (peeled and cubed)
- 3 cloves garlic (minced)
- 2 teaspoon ground black pepper (crushed)
- 1 teaspoon sugar
- 1 tablespoon soy sauce
- 1 teaspoon rice vinegar
- 1 tablespoon vegetable oil
- Parsley for garnish (coarsely chopped)

Utensils Needed:

- Wok
- Spatula
- Cutting board
- Cleaver

Directions:

Peel pumpkin after washing with cold running water. Remove the seeds and cut into cubes. Peel the garlic and mince.

Turn on the stove and put a wok. Over medium flame, put 1 tablespoon of vegetable oil. Wait until hot, then add the garlic. Sauté until garlic turns slightly brown. Put 500 grams of cubed pumpkin and stir-fry until it turns a little bit tender. Drizzle with black pepper, soy sauce, rice vinegar and sugar. Stir frequently until all ingredients are well mixed. Be careful not to let the pumpkin get too soft. Serves 3-4 persons. Garnish with parsley.

Health Tip:

- Black pepper is good for digestion. Adding black pepper in your recipe will prevent you from having constipation or diarrhea.

- Rice vinegar do the same thing. It helps in proper digestion since it contains high amount of acetic acid, which improves the absorption of food in the body.

Fried chili potatoes with green bell pepper

Ingredients:

- 450 grams potatoes (peeled and sliced)
- 1 large green bell pepper (cut into strips)
- 1 tablespoon cornstarch
- 2 tablespoon cold water
- 3 tablespoon vegetable oil
- 1 medium onion (cut into strips)
- 4 small cloves garlic (minced)
- 2 tablespoon soy sauce
- 1 tablespoon hot chili sauce
- 1 teaspoon paprika powder
- Salt and pepper to taste
- 2 teaspoon spring onion (chopped for garnish)

Utensils Needed:

- Wok
- Spatula
- Cutting board
- Cleaver
- Peeler
- Small mixing bowl

Directions:

Prepare 450 grams of potatoes peeled and washed with cold water. Peel the skin of the potatoes using a peeler then slice. Wash 1 large green bell pepper and cut into strips. DO not remove the seeds. Wash garlic and onion and peel them. Mince the garlic and slice the onion into strips. Set them aside.

Combine 1 tablespoon of cornstarch and 2 tablespoons of cold water in a mixing bowl. Dissolve the cornstarch well into the water.

In a wok, put 3 tablespoons of vegetable oil. Wait until oil is hot before putting garlic and onion. Sauté for 1 minute then add the potatoes. Stir-fry until potatoes turn golden brown. Add the green bell pepper and stir fry until slightly tender. Pour 2 tablespoon of soy sauce, 1 teaspoon of rice vinegar and 1 tablespoon of hot chili sauce into the wok. Coat the potatoes with the liquid seasoning. Add the cornstarch mixture and let it simmer. Sprinkle a teaspoon of paprika powder and pinch of salt and pepper. Continue stir-frying for 2-3 minutes. Serve hot to 3-4 person.

Health Tip:

- Paprika contains iron that helps in forming more red blood cells in the body. Mixing paprika in your recipe will prevent you from getting iron deficiency anemia.

Mushroom with Chinese agave nectar sauce

Ingredients:

- 450 grams shiitake mushroom (sliced)
- 3 tablespoon agave nectar
- ¼ cup vegetable broth
- 1 teaspoon rice vinegar
- 1 teaspoon sherry
- 2 teaspoon ginger (diced)
- 1 tablespoon olive oil
- 1 teaspoon cornstarch
- 1 tablespoon light soy sauce

Utensils Needed:

- Wok
- Spatula
- Cutting board
- Cleaver

Directions:

Remove the mushroom stem after cleaning with water and cut the mushroom caps into halves. Cut the ginger after peeling into cubes.

Heat a wok and put 1 tablespoon of olive oil. Stir-fry the mushroom and ginger for 2-3 minutes and add ¼ cup of vegetable broth. Pour 3 tablespoon of agave nectar and let it simmer. Put a teaspoon of cornstarch and allow the sauce to thicken. Stir occasionally. Add the other ingredients starting with soy sauce, then vinegar and sherry. Let it cook for another 2-3 minutes then serve to 3-4 persons.

Celery and Carrot Chinese Salad

Ingredients:

- 250 grams celery (trimmed and cut into thin strips)
- 250 grams carrots (peeled and cut into thin strips)
- 1 garlic clove (minced)
- 2 tablespoon light soy sauce
- 2 tablespoon olive oil
- 1 teaspoon apple cider vinegar
- 1 teaspoon Shaoxing wine
- 1 teaspoon salt
- 1 teaspoon black pepper powder
- 1 teaspoon agave nectar

Utensils Needed:

- Large mixing bowl
- Cleaver
- Cutting board
- Pot
- Colander
- Two wooden spoon

Directions:

Clean and trim celery stalks and cut into thin strips. Wash, peel and cut the carrots. Peel the ginger and mince. Set them aside.

In a large mixing bowl, pour all seasoning. Put 2 tablespoon of light soy sauce, 2 tablespoons of olive oil, a teaspoon of apple cider vinegar and Shaoxing wine. Whisk until combine. Then add a teaspoon of agave nectar, pepper and salt. Save for later use.

In a pot of boiling water, put carrots and celery. Cook until vegetables are al dente. Then drain using a colander and rinse with cold running water. Pat to dry.

Toss the vegetables into the liquid mixture using two wooden spoon. Coat the vegetables well with the salad dressing. Serve cold to 4 persons.

Health Tip:

- Having sleepless nights and stressful days? You should start having celery for snack or add it in your meals, and you will be having a good night sleep and calm days. Celery contains high amount of magnesium and calcium, which has relaxing effect in the nervous system.

Chinese Cabbage Noodle soup with Carrots

Ingredients:

- 120 grams noodles
- 300 grams cabbage (shredded)
- 200 grams carrots (diced)
- 100 grams chickpeas
- 4 cups vegetable broth
- 2 tablespoon soy sauce
- 1 tablespoon vegetable oil
- 1 medium size onion (chopped)
- 2 cloves garlic (minced)
- 1 teaspoon salt
- 1 teaspoon dried thyme
- Chopped parsley for garnish

Utensils Needed:

- Pot
- Hoak
- Cleaver
- Cutting board

Directions:

Prepare the vegetables and clean with cold running water. Peel and dice the carrots. Cut the cabbage into thin strips. Peel garlic and onion and then mince. Clean chickpeas with cold water and pat to dry so the skin can be remove easily. Set vegetables aside.

Heat pot and put vegetable oil. Stir-fry onion and garlic then add the carrots. Continue stirring until carrots are al dente. Pour 4 cups of vegetable broth and let it boil. Add the noodles and chickpeas. Put 2 tablespoon of soy sauce, 1 teaspoon of salt and dried thyme. Then add the cabbage. Cover the pot and bring to simmer. Do not overcook the vegetable and noodles. Pour in a bowl using a hoak and garnish with chopped parsley and serve hot to 2 persons.

Health Tip:

- Chickpeas is one of the good source of protein among vegetarians. Eating chickpeas will provide you certain amino acids that the body needs.

Mixed Mushroom Chinese Recipe
Ingredients:

- 500 grams of different mushroom (oyster, shiitake, enoki, Portobello, shimeji)
- 3 tablespoon vegetable oil
- 3 tablespoon light soy sauce
- 1 teaspoon apple cider vinegar
- 1 teaspoon garlic powder
- 1 teaspoon ginger powder
- 1 bunch spring onions (chopped)
- Pepper to taste

Utensils Needed:

- Wok
- Spatula
- Cutting board
- Cleaver

Directions:

Clean each mushroom with cold water and dry with paper towel. Cut each mushroom into pieces. It depends on your preference, if you want cube, julienne or cut into halves.

Put 3 tablespoon of vegetable oil in a wok. Let oil shimmer before adding the mushroom. Add 3 tablespoon of soy sauce, a teaspoon of garlic, ginger powder, apple cider vinegar into the wok and combine well with the mushroom. Stir-fry for about 3 minutes until mushrooms are cooked. Season with pepper and spring onions. Serve warm to 4 persons.

Health Tip:

- Apple cider vinegar is termed as a miracle cure for various diseases that is why it is known to give people longer life. Adding cider in your recipe will give you multiple health benefits. This includes lowers blood cholesterol level, prevents and fights cancer cells, helps you lose weight, fights off infection, reduces blood sugar level, keeps healthy skin, helps wound healing, improves different organ function and maintains a healthy heart.

Sweet and Sour Baked Tofu

Ingredients:

- 400 grams tofu (sliced)
- 1 tablespoon soy sauce
- 3 tablespoon sugar
- 2 tablespoon lime juice
- 1 tablespoon rice vinegar
- 2 tablespoon sesame oil
- 1 teaspoon garlic (minced)
- 1 teaspoon ginger (minced)
- ½ teaspoon salt
- ½ teaspoon pepper

Utensils Needed:

- Oven
- Baking pan
- Large mixing bowl
- Cleaver
- Cutting board

Directions:

Remove excess water from tofu by pressing. Slice into desired shape. Set Aside. Peel ginger and garlic, then mince. Save for later use.

In a large mixing bowl, combine all seasoning. Put 2 tablespoon of sesame oil, 2 tablespoons of lemon juice, 1 tablespoon of rice vinegar, and 3 tablespoon of sugar. Mix until sugar dissolves. Add a teaspoon of minced ginger and garlic. Season with half a teaspoon of salt and pepper. Whisk thoroughly. Now, carefully put the sliced tofu and soak overnight or can be bake right away.

Preheat oven to 375°F. Place tofu in a nonstick baking pan. Bake for 20-30 minutes until cooked. Serve on top of rice to 4 persons.

Health Tip:

- Fresh lemon juice is a powerful detoxifying agent for the body. It helps get rid of bacteria and viruses, removes toxins, keep the digestive system healthy and enhance immune system function.

Chinese Sweet Scallion Pancake

Ingredients:

- 2 cups chopped spring onions
- 2 cups all-purpose flour
- 1 cup warm water
- ½ tablespoon salt
- 2 tablespoon granulated sugar
- Caster sugar (for baking sheet)
- Olive oil for brushing
- 2 tablespoon vegetable oil for frying

Utensils Needed:

- Wok
- Cleaver
- Cutting board
- Baking sheet
- Oil brush
- Wooden rolling pin
- Spatula
- Bowl and plastic to cover bowl

Directions:

In a mixing bowl, put 2 cups of all-purpose flour. Pour warm water and combine well with the flour. Knead until dough is smooth. Cover the bowl and let it sit for an hour.

Clean spring onions and chop into small pieces. Set aside.

On a baking sheet, sprinkle caster sugar. This will prevent the dough to stick on the baking sheet. Place the dough and roll to flatten. Cut into 8 parts of equally square shaped dough. Sprinkle spring onions on the dough and season with a pinch of salt and ½ teaspoon of sugar. Make sure to distribute sugar evenly on the dough. Brush every side of the dough with olive oil. Roll the dough into log shape then coil to form a round dough. Flatten the round dough with a rolling pin. Always dust caster sugar when doing the dough on the baking sheet to avoid the dough from sticking on it.

Heat 2 tablespoon of vegetable oil in a wok. Wait until oil is hot before placing the pancakes. Flip each side of the pancake to cook both side. Fry each side until slightly brown. Serve warm to 8 people.

Health Tip:

- Olive oil is best for human heart. It prevents certain cardiovascular disease due to accumulation of bad cholesterol in the body. Olive oil boost good cholesterol while eliminating bad cholesterol in the body. This makes olive oil one of the best oil for frying food or even for making salad dishes.

Chili Garlic Spinach with oyster sauce
Ingredients:

- 350 grams spinach
- 2 tablespoon oyster sauce
- 4 cloves garlic (chopped)
- 1 large onion (chopped)
- 5 dried red chili pepper (minced)
- 1 tablespoon vegetable oil
- 1 teaspoon sugar
- 1 teaspoon rice vinegar
- Pepper to taste

Utensils Needed:

- Wok
- Spatula
- Cleaver
- Cutting board

Directions:

Clean spinach with water, then let it dry. Remove the large and hard stem at the bottom part of the spinach. Peel garlic and onion, then chopped. Remove the seeds of dried red chili pepper and mince.

Pour 1 tablespoon of vegetable oil in a heated wok. Add the garlic, onion and dried chili pepper into the wok. Sauté for a minute or just until you can smell the aroma of the spices. Add the spinach and toss using a spatula to mix with the seasoning. Put 2 tablespoon of oyster sauce and a teaspoon of rice vinegar and sugar into the wok. Stir-fry until spinach leaves are wilted or stems are tender. Season with pepper to taste. Serve warm to 3-4 person.

Health Tip:

- A combination of garlic and onion in a dish

keeps the body from acquiring heart problems. These two popular ingredients in many recipes are relatives not just scientifically but also in helping people fight heart illnesses. They contain substances that allows smooth circulation of blood throughout the body and thus preventing clot formation, which is one reason why heart attack happens.

Chinese Vegan Dumpling Soup

Ingredients:

- 20 vegetarian wonton wrapper
- 1/4 cup carrots (minced)
- 1/2 cup cabbage (coarsely chopped)
- ¼ cup mushroom (finely chopped)
- 2-inch ginger (grated)
- 2 tablespoon soy sauce
- 1 tablespoon sesame oil
- 1 teaspoon of dried thyme
- 1 teaspoon salt (for soup) and 2 teaspoon salt (for mixed vegetables)
- 1 teaspoon fine black pepper and 2 teaspoon pepper (for mixed vegetables)
- 4 cups vegetable broth
- 1 bunch scallions (chopped)

Utensils Needed:

- Large pot
- Hoak
- Cutting board
- Cleaver

Directions:

Clean all vegetables and finely chop. Put in a large mixing bowl. Sprinkle with salt and pepper. Mix well. Prepare your wonton wrapper and put a tablespoon of mixed vegetables in the center of the wrapper. Wrap the vegetable into desired shape. Set aside.

Turn your stove over medium flame and heat a large pot of vegetable broth. Put your dumplings and ginger into the broth, then let it boil. Add 2 tablespoon of soy sauce and a tablespoon of sesame oil. Season with a teaspoon of dried thyme, salt and pepper. Cover and bring to simmer. Sprinkle chopped scallions and serve hot to 4

persons.

Health Tip:

- Are you having stress related acne and looking for a home remedy? One of the benefits that thyme gives is treating infection and improving temperament. Thyme has both anti-bacterial properties that can prevent and treat acne. Furthermore, it contains substance that promotes neuron activity, which stimulates good mood.

Stir-fried Cabbage and Carrot Recipe

Ingredients:

- 500 grams cabbage (shredded)
- 250 grams carrots (cut into thin strips)
- 1 medium size red bell pepper and green bell pepper (sliced thinly)
- 1 tablespoon light soy sauce
- 1 teaspoon Chinese black vinegar
- 1 teaspoon garlic powder
- 1 teaspoon onion powder
- Salt and pepper to taste
- 1 tablespoon of vegetable oil

Utensils Needed:

- Wok
- Spatula
- Cleaver
- Cutting board

Directions: Wash cabbage and carrots. Shred the cabbage and julienne the carrots. Slice the bell pepper into thin strips after washing. Set aside.

Heat a wok over medium flame and put 1 tablespoon of vegetable oil. Add the vegetable and stir-fry until cook. Put the carrots first, followed by the cabbage and bell pepper. Pour soy sauce and vinegar. Season with garlic and onion powder. Toss the vegetables to coat with all the seasonings. Sprinkle with a pinch of salt and pepper. Serve warm to 2 persons.

Health Tip:

- Did you know that Chinese black vinegar is one of the most natural way of relieving muscle pain. If you happen to exert too much effort in your workout and feel in pain. Prepare a dish with Chinese black vinegar and it can solve your pain problem.

Stir-fried Vegetable Rice Noodles

Ingredients:

- 250 grams rice noodles
- 50 grams baby corns
- 50 grams carrots (cut into thin strips)
- 50 grams green peas
- 50 grams red bell pepper (cut into thin strips)
- 2 tablespoon soy sauce
- 2 cloves garlic (minced)
- 1 small size onion (minced)
- 2 tablespoon vegetable oil
- Salt and pepper to taste
- Water for boiling noodles

Utensils Needed:

- Pot (for cooking noodles)
- Wok
- Spatula
- Cutting board
- Cleaver
- Colander

Directions:

Prepare all vegetables. Clean green peas and remove skin. Cut the carrots and red bell pepper into thin strips. Cut the baby corn into halves. Peel the garlic and onion, then mince. Set all vegetables aside.

In a pot of boiling water. Cook noodles until al dente. Drain using a colander and set aside.

Prepare a wok and put 2 tablespoons of vegetable oil. When oil shimmers, sauté the garlic and onion. Add the vegetables and stir-fry until tender. Now, add the cooked noodles and toss all ingredients well. Pour soy sauce and sprinkle with salt and pepper. Stir continuously for a minute and serve to 2 persons.

Health Tip:

- One of the health benefit that baby corns provide is greatly for pregnant women. If suffering from nausea and vomiting, which is common during early pregnancy. Add some baby corns in your meal and you don't have to worry about the morning sickness feeling.

Chinese Vegetable Salad with Fruits

Ingredients:

- 450 grams chickpeas
- 100 grams cucumber (sliced)
- 100 grams apple (sliced)
- 50 grams cranberries
- 1 large onion (sliced)
- 1 medium size red bell pepper (cut into strips)
- 50 grams lettuce (coarsely chopped)
- 2 thin slice of orange for garnish
- 3 tablespoon Chinese black vinegar
- 1 teaspoon sugar
- 2 tablespoon olive oil
- 1 teaspoon salt
- 1 teaspoon pepper

Utensils Needed:

- Large mixing bowl
- 2 wooden spoon
- Cutting board
- Cleaver
- Pot for cooking chickpeas

Directions:

In a large pot of boiling water, cook chickpeas. Drain and rinse with water. Set aside for later use.

Wash vegetables and fruits properly with clean, cold water. Make sure to use organic vegetables and fruits if you don't want to remove their peelings. Cut vegetables and fruits into desired shape. Coarsely chop lettuce. Save for later use.

In a large mixing bowl, prepare the salad dressing. Mix 3 tablespoon of black vinegar and 2 tablespoons of olive oil. Add 1 teaspoon of sugar and a teaspoon of salt and pepper. Combine all liquid and dry ingredients well. Put the vegetables and fruits in the dressing. Toss using two wooden spoon and completely coat all fruits and vegetables with the dressing. Garnish with orange slices. Serve cold to two persons.

Health Tip:

- If you want high doses of vitamins, eat a bunch of lettuce for salad. It has good source of vitamin A, vitamin C, B-carotene, folate and vitamin K. These crucial vitamins are essential in keeping the body healthy and in fighting of infection and diseases such as Cancer.
- Do you want to avoid getting urinary tract infection? One of the best natural solution is eating cranberries. It contains a substance called Proanthocyanins that helps prevent bacteria from attacking the urinary tract system.

Chinese Mushroom Soup

Ingredients:

- 250 grams shiitake mushroom (cut into halves)
- 6 cups of vegetable broth
- 2-inch ginger (grated)
- 2 cloves garlic (minced)
- 2 tablespoon soy sauce
- 1 tablespoon rice vinegar
- 1 tablespoon vegetable oil
- Salt to taste
- Chopped Scallions and parsley for garnish

Utensils Needed:

- Large pot
- Cutting board
- Cleaver
- Hoak

Directions:

Clean the mushroom and remove the stems. Cut the caps into halves. Mince garlic and grate the ginger.

In a large pot, put 1 tablespoon of vegetable oil. Sauté garlic until slightly brown then add the mushroom. Stir-fry for 1 minute. Just enough to mix the garlic with the mushroom. Pour 6 cups of vegetable broth and add the ginger. Cover the pot and let it boil. Add soy sauce and vinegar. Season with salt and let it simmer. Sprinkle with scallions and parsley and serve hot to 4 persons.

Health Tip:

- In preparing vegetable broth, it is best not to include salt in the vegetables. This will add more sodium in the broth, which is not good for the health. Just plainly boil organic vegetables and keep it natural without adding condiments. This will keep more vitamins and less sodium that is better for human health.

Spicy Sesame Seed Balls

Ingredients:

- 400 grams glutinous rice flour
- 50 grams sesame seed
- 250 grams hot red bean paste
- 150 grams sugar
- 300 ml boiling water
- 5 cups of vegetable oil

Utensils Needed:

- Wok
- Strainer
- Mixing bowls
- Pot

Directions:

Boil 300 ml of water using a pot, then dissolve 150 grams of sugar in it. Set aside.

Prepare sesame seeds and put in a bowl. Set aside.

In a mixing bowl, prepare the glutinous flour. Mix in the sugar mixture and completely combine the ingredients. You should have a sticky dough after mixing thoroughly. Get a spoonful of the dough and flatten it, put a teaspoon or two of hot red bean paste in the center of the dough. Cover the bean paste completely with the sticky dough.

Before frying, roll the dough in the bowl of sesame seeds. Once completely covered with seeds. Put in a wok with 5 cups of hot vegetable oil. Make sure the oil is hot before frying. Cook until the balls turn golden brown. Once cook, get the sesame seed balls by using a strainer. Place in a plate with paper towel to remove excess oil. Serves about 45 sesame seed balls.

Health Tip:

- Red bean paste is a good source of antioxidant, which means it can help you fight off against cancer cells.

Fried Baby Corns with Schezuan dipping sauce

Ingredients:

- 250 grams baby corns
- ½ cup corn flour
- ½ tsp chili powder
- ¼ cup of water
- ½ teaspoon curry powder
- Pinch of salt and pepper
- Enough vegetable oil for deep frying about 1-2 cups
- 6 red dried chili pepper (minced)
- 1 tablespoon garlic (minced)
- 1 teaspoon sugar
- ½ tsp salt (for sauce)
- 2 tablespoon vinegar
- 1 tablespoon sesame oil

Utensils Needed:

- Wok
- Cutting board
- Cleaver
- Mixing bowls
- Wooden spoon
- Spatula
- Strainer

Directions:

Prepare the baby corns. Wash with clean water. Cut into halves. Mince the garlic and red dried chili pepper. Set aside.

In a mixing bowl, whisk red dried chili pepper, sugar, vinegar, garlic, salt and sesame oil. Mix thoroughly and save for later use as a dipping sauce.

In a separate mixing bowl, combine corn flour, chili powder, curry powder, salt, pepper, and ¼ cup of water. Mix until all ingredients are dissolved. Soak the baby corns into the corn flour mixture.

Heat wok over medium flame. Put enough amount of oil for deep-frying. When oil is hot, add garlic and baby corns. Stir-fry until golden brown. Using a strainer, drain the baby corns of any excess oil. Place in a plate with paper towels. Serve with Schezuan dipping sauce. Serves 2-3 persons.

Health Tip:

- Per studies, curcumin, which is found in turmeric, prevents diseases like Alzheimer. This substance helps in eliminating plaque formation that causes cognitive problems.

Chinese Black Sesame Coconut Vegan Ice Cream

Ingredients:

- 1 cup coconut milk
- ¼ cup maple syrup
- 2 teaspoon vanilla extract
- 1/8 teaspoon of spirulina
- 80 grams of toasted black sesame powder
- 1/8 teaspoon salt

Utensils Needed:

- Blender
- wok for toasting black sesame seed
- spatula
- Sealed container

Directions:

In a wok, put 80 grams of black sesame seed. Fry until toasted. Let it cool before putting it in a blender.

Prepare blender. Put the toasted black sesame seed and blend until it turned to powder. Now add 1 cup of coconut milk and ¼ cup of maple syrup. Blend until pureed. Add spirulina, salt and vanilla extract. Blend until smooth. Pour mixture in a sealed plastic container. Freeze overnight. Serve cold to 5 persons.

Health Tip:

- Spirulina is considered one of the most powerful detoxifying natural agent. It can treat food poisoning caused by arsenic. Studies showed that due to its substances, it could remove toxic waste from the body.

Fried Bananas with cinnamon and sesame seeds

Ingredients:

- 200 grams bananas (peeled and sliced)
- 120 ml water
- 4 tablespoon all-purpose flour
- 4 tablespoon corn flour
- Pinch of baking powder
- Oil for deep frying
- 80 grams sugar
- 1 teaspoon cinnamon
- 2 tablespoon water
- 1 teaspoon sesame seed

Utensils Needed:

- Wok
- Sauce pan
- Spatula
- Cutting board
- Cleaver
- Mixing bowl
- Strainer

Directions:

Peel the bananas and slice into desired shape. Set them aside.

Combine 120ml water, all-purpose flour and corn flour. Sprinkle with a pinch of baking powder. Stir thoroughly until smooth. Get your bananas and coat with the flour mixture.

In a saucepan, combine 2 tablespoons of water, sugar, and cinnamon. Wait until sugar dissolve and thickens.

In a wok, heat oil just enough for deep-frying. Add the flour-coated bananas and deep fry until golden brown. Remove from the wok using a strainer to discard excess oil then dip into sugar mixture. Place in a plate then sprinkle with sesame seeds. Serve warm to 2 persons.

Health Tip:

- Bananas has high amount of potassium that helps in keeping a healthy heart. One banana a day will keep you from developing heart related diseases.

Vege-Thai-Rian

Ariya Netjoy Presents:

VEGANIZED

FILIPINO VEGAN FEAST

BE GOOD AND KIND TO ALL LIVING BEINGS
PRACTICE IT

Copyrights 2017 All rights reserved © Ariya Netjoy

No part of this publication or the information in it may be quoted from or reproduced in any form by means such as printing, scanning, photocopying, or otherwise without prior written permission of the copyright holder.

Sunny Thai Publishing

Terms of Use Disclaimer Efforts have been made to ensure that the information in this book is accurate. However, the author and the publisher do not hold any responsibility for errors, omissions, or contrary interpretation of the subject matter herein. The recipes provided in this book are for informational purposes only and are not intended to provide dietary advice. A medical practitioner should be consulted for dietary advice. Additionally, recipe cooking times may require adjustment depending on age and quality of appliances and tools. Readers are urged to take all needed precautions to ensure ingredients are fully cooked to avoid the dangers of foodborne illnesses. The author and publisher do not take any responsibility for any consequences that may result due to following the instructions provided in this book.

Thank you for being a loyal reader and friend. As a reward, we would like to bring even more delicious vegan and vegetarian dishes into your life, FREE! All you must do, is sign up with your email and you are set. Everything is free and full of fun so come on and eat with us! Click the blue mail above. Available on the Kindle version.

Table of Contents

Introduction

Fried Vegetable (Lumpia) Spring Roll

Champorado or Sweet Chocolate Rice Porridge

Vegetarian Halo-Halo (Mixed fruits, beans and vegetable dessert)

Monggo (Mung) Beans with Malunggay (Horseradish) Leaves Soup

String Beans with Tofu Adobo (cooked in vinegar, soy sauce and garlic)

Sautéed Calabash

Pancit Bihon (Rice Vermicelli or Bijon Noodle) Recipe

Spicy Taro Leaves with Coconut Milk (Laing)

Boiled Mix Vegetables (Bulanglang)

Stir-Fried Pumpkin with Long Beans

Coconut Pandan Vegan Dessert

Seaweed Salad

Fresh Spring Rolls

Fried Eggplant with Spicy Sauce

Jackfruit in Coconut Milk

Eggplant Salad

Water Spinach Adobo (cooked in vinegar, soy sauce and garlic)

Creamy Coconut Papaya with Horseradish Leaves

Garlic Fried Rice

Caramelized Sweet Potatoes

Squash with Bitter Melon Leaves Soup

Fruit Salad Filipino Style

Vermicelli Noodle (Misua) with Sponge Gourd

Sautéed Cabbage with Mushroom

Tofu in Thick Tomato Sauce

Mixed Vegetables in Tamarind Soup

Creamy Macaroni Pasta Soup with Mixed Vegetables

Vegetable Curry Filipino Style

Rice Purple Yam Cake in Bamboo Tube (Puto Bumbong)

Spicy and Hot Garlic Beans with Coconut Milk

Radish Salad Filipino Style

Sautéed Bok Choy (Pechay) in Vinegar, Garlic and Soy Sauce

Banana Blossoms in Creamy Coconut Sauce

Coconut Corn Pudding (Maja Blanca)

Rice Porridge with Tofu

Bitter Gourd Salad Filipino Style

Coleslaw Filipino Style

Cassava with Grated Coconut Dessert

Asparagus Soup Filipino Style

Sweet and Sour Tofu with Mixed Vegetables

Broccoli in Spicy Sauce

Garlic Mushroom with Vegan Soy Sauce and Vinegar

Corn Soup

Bamboo Shoot Adobo (cooked in Soy Sauce, Vinegar and Garlic)

Cabbage Soup Filipino Style

Cauliflower with Carrots in Thick Garlic Sauce

Mung Beans Coconut Popsicle

Sticky Rice Balls with Jack Fruit Recipe

Potato Chips Filipino Recipe

Steamed Brown Rice Cake with Grated Coconut

Introduction

Filipino vegetarian dishes are a blend of both Asian and Western cuisines. In the past, different races from all over the world conquered the Philippine archipelago. This includes Chinese, Malaysian, Indonesian, Japanese, Americans and Spaniards. They made a great impact to Filipinos way of cooking in the past and until now, the hint of foreign taste is part of many Filipino recipes.

When different nationalities occupied the country, they introduced different varieties of food to ancient Filipinos. Soy sauce, tofu, and noodles came from Chinese and Japanese cuisines. Curry and rice cakes are influenced by Indonesians and Malaysians. Spaniards brought the use of different spices like garlic, onions, chili peppers and tomatoes, while Americans introduced ice cream and ketchup to Filipino cuisines.

The famous adobo or cooked with vinegar, soy sauce and garlic is a combination of different cookery and is now a well-known Filipino dish in the world. Traditionally, adobo is made from cooking chicken or pork with vinegar, soy sauce, and garlic, but Filipinos are naturally creative in making vegetarian dishes. These days, Adobo can be prepared by using different vegetables like water spinach, eggplants and string beans.

Through the years, the Filipino cuisine has evolved into its own unique vegetarian delicacies and is now being enjoyed by the locals. Even tourists from different countries relish every Filipino recipe whenever they visit the country.

In this cookbook, you will appreciate different vegan recipes that are creatively made by Filipinos and you will surely love it.

Fried Vegetable (Lumpia) Spring Roll

Ingredients:

- 500 grams bean sprouts
- 25 pieces vegan spring roll wrappers
- 1 large carrot (diced)
- 3 shallots (minced)
- 3 cloves garlic (minced)
- 200 grams shredded green cabbage
- A bunch of spring onions (chopped)
- ½ teaspoon salt
- ½ teaspoon pepper
- Vegetable oil for frying
- 2 teaspoon light soy sauce

Utensils Needed:

- Kawali or wok (kawali is a Filipino term for wok or skillet)
- Spatula
- Chopping board
- Kitchen knife

Directions:

Prepare your vegetables and wash with water. Pat them to dry. Peel the skin of carrots, shallots and garlic. Cut carrots into small pieces. Mince both garlic and onion. Chop the spring onions and using a kitchen knife, slice green cabbage into small pieces. Snap off dark or dried end of bean sprouts. Set them aside.

Heat oil in a wok. Sauté minced garlic and shallots. When shallots turn translucent, add bean sprouts, green cabbage carrots and spring onions in the wok. Now, pour 2 teaspoon of light soy sauce and season with half a teaspoon of salt and pepper. Stir the vegetable until tender.

Get 25 pieces of spring roll wrappers. Place 2-3 tablespoon of sautéed vegetable diagonally on the corner of the wrapper. Fold firmly until it comes to the other end. Secure each corner while folding. You can wet all sides of the wrapper with water to make sure they stick together when folding.

Prepare vegetable oil in a wok enough for deep-frying. Turn stove on medium flame and deep-fry 25 vegetable spring rolls. Cook until golden. Serve with light soy sauce or ketchup as dipping sauce to 4 persons.

Health Tips:
- If you want a natural cure for stomach problems, then you should include spring onions in your recipe. It's a rich source of fiber that helps in good digestion. Spring onions can also enhance your appetite.

Champorado or Sweet Chocolate Rice Porridge

Ingredients:

- 500 grams glutinous rice
- 6 cups of water
- ½ cup cocoa powder
- ¼ cup chocolate tablea or chopped chocolate bar
- ½ cup sugar (you can use brown sugar)
- Almond milk or Coconut milk (garnish)

Utensils Needed:

- Palayok or Clay pot
- Ladle
- Kalan (clay stove)
- Coal for cooking

Directions:

Wash 500 grams of glutinous rice with water. Rinse at least 2 to 3 times. Drain excess water. Prepare other ingredients for the rice porridge.

Prepare a clay stove and put some coal inside. When coal is in medium flame. Place clay pot on top of the stove. Put 500 grams of washed glutinous rice into the clay pot. Pour 6 cups of water and cover the pot. Let it boil. After 20 minutes, reduce burned coals to lower the heat. Stir the rice constantly to avoid sticking on the bottom of the pot. Add ½ cup of cocoa powder and ¼ cup of chopped chocolate bar and mix well with the rice. Dissolve ½ cup of sugar and using a ladle, combine all the ingredients together. Bring to simmer. Transfer to a bowl and pour almond milk or coconut milk on top. Server warm to 4-5 persons.

Health Tips:
- Almond milk comes from almond nuts or almond butter mix with water producing a liquid mixture. It is one of the best alternative milk for vegans. It's dairy-free and low in calories. According to many studies, almond nuts keep your heart strong. It prevents you from getting heart attacks and acquiring cardiovascular problems. Oleic acid, one component of almonds lowers bad cholesterol in the body, and thus maintaining your heart healthy.

Vegetarian Halo-Halo (Mixed fruits, beans and vegetable dessert)

Ingredients:

- 1 cup coconut milk or almond milk
- Shaved ice
- 1 can coconut gel
- 1 can sugar palm fruit
- ½ cup Purple yam jam
- 1 cup Sweetened banana
- 1 cup Flavored gelatin
- ¼ cup Rice flakes
- 1 cup Sweetened red beans
- ½ cup sweetened jackfruit (shredded)
- 1 cup Coconut fruit (shredded)
- Ice cream of choice

Utensils Needed:

- Ice shaver/crusher
- Tall glass or deep bowls
- Spoon
- Shredder (for coconut fruit and jackfruit)

Directions:

Prepare all your ingredients. You can buy a can of mixed fruits as well if you want to make simple halo-halo.

Get 5-6 tall clear glasses or transparent deep bowls. Get a spoon and add 2-3 tablespoons of each ingredients in each glasses or bowls. Start with 2-3 tablespoons of sweetened red beans, then 2-3 tablespoons of coconut gel, sugar palm fruit, sweetened banana, flavored gelatin, and shredded coconut fruit. Then, using an Ice crusher, shave your ice. Put shaved ice on each glasses or bowls. Leave enough space on top of the shaved ice to put the other ingredients. Now, get a scoop of ice cream and place on top of the shaved ice. Filipinos prefer purple yam ice cream for halo-halo. Add on the side of the ice cream a tablespoon of purple yam jam, sweetened banana, flavored gelatin, coconut gel, sugar palm fruit, red beans and jackfruit. Sprinkle with 2 teaspoon of rice flakes and finally pour 4 to 5 tablespoons of almond milk or coconut milk. Serve to 5-6 persons.

For authentic feeling, you have to mix all the ingredients before eating, but some people prefer eating the ice cream first.

Health Tips:
- Purple yam is actually a root vegetable. It contains potassium that regulates normal blood pressure. Potassium also helps in giving your body energy to recover after working out. Eating purple yam increases your stamina, while keeping your blood pressure regulated normally.

Monggo (Mung) Beans with Malunggay (Horseradish) Leaves Soup

Ingredients:

- 1 cup monggo (mung) beans
- ½ cup malunggay (horseradish) leaves (trimmed)
- 4 cups vegetable broth
- 5 cups water
- 3 cloves garlic (minced)
- 1 medium size onion (minced)
- 2-inch ginger (minced)
- 1 large tomato (sliced)
- 2 teaspoon salt
- ½ cup coconut milk
- 1 teaspoon pepper
- 1 tablespoon vegetable oil

Utensils Needed:

- Pot
- Saucepan
- Ladle
- Kitchen knife
- Chopping board
- Strainer/colander

Directions:

Rinse horseradish leaves, tomato, onion and garlic with water. Soak mung beans with water, discard floating beans and drain water. Chop onions and garlic into small pieces, and then slice the tomato. Set aside.

Put 1 cup of mung beans in a pot. Add 5 cups of water. Turn stove on medium flame and cover the pot. Bring to boil and cook until soft. Using a strainer, discard water.

Sauté minced garlic and onions in a saucepan with hot oil. Season with salt and pepper. Add sliced tomato stir-fry.

Put softened mung beans into the saucepan. Pour 4 cups of vegetable broth. Mix well and then cover the pan. Let it simmer and then add the horseradish leaves. Cook for another 10 minutes. Serve hot to 4 persons.

Health Tips:
- Malunggay leaves as commonly known in the Philippines or Horseradish leaves in English can lower blood sugar level in the body among diabetic persons.
- Mung beans on the other hand is a great source of protein among plants. It contains about 20-24% of amino acids like leucine, valine and isoleucine. It's a good protein alternative for vegetarians.

String Beans with Tofu Adobo (cooked in vinegar, soy sauce and garlic)

Ingredients:

- 500 grams string beans (trimmed and cut into 2 inches long)
- 250 grams tofu (diced)
- 1 cup vegetable broth
- 5 tablespoon vinegar
- 7 tablespoon vegan soy sauce (use tamari brand)
- 6 cloves garlic (chopped)
- 1 large onion (sliced)
- 1 teaspoon powdered black pepper
- 2 tablespoon vegetable oil

Utensils Needed:

- Wok or frying pan
- Spatula
- Kitchen knife
- Chopping board

Directions:

Wash string beans with water and trim. Cut into 2 inches long. Drain tofu and chop into cubes. Peel onion and garlic skin and slice using a kitchen knife. Set them aside.

Turn stove to medium flame and put a frying pan on top of it. Heat 2 tablespoon of vegetable oil. Sauté garlic and onion. When garlic turns brown, add string beans and tofu. Stir until tofu is golden and string beans are tender. Pour soy sauce and vinegar. Add a cup of vegetable broth and bring to simmer. Season with salt and pepper. Mix well using a spatula. Serve warm with rice to 4 to 5 persons.

Health Tips:

- String beans are loaded of vitamin K. This vitamin is essential in taking up calcium in the body to keep your bone strong. Without vitamin K, even if you have stored plenty calcium in your body. You won't gain healthier bones.

Sautéed Calabash

Ingredients:

- 400 grams calabash or bottle gourd (peeled and sliced thinly)
- 3 cloves garlic (minced)
- 3-4 dried red chili
- 1 teaspoon pepper
- 2 teaspoon salt
- 2 tablespoon vegetable oil

Utensils Needed:

- Frying pan or wok
- Spatula
- Chopping board
- Kitchen knife

Directions:

Wash calabash or bottle gourd with water and then remove the skin. Chop into thinly slices. Remove the husk of garlic after washing then mince. Mince 4 dried red chili and save for later use.

Put 2 tablespoon of vegetable oil in a wok or frying pan. Heat over medium flame. When oil is shimmering, add garlic. Then, add sliced calabash and minced red chili. Sauté until calabash is tender. Season with salt and pepper. Serve warm to 3-4 persons.

Health Tips:

- If you're planning to lose some weight, then you

should be making recipes out of bottle gourd or calabash. This vegetable has low calorie count and is good for your body because it contains vitamin C and B, which helps your cell fights free radical damage and improve your cognitive ability.

Pancit Bihon (Rice Vermicelli or Bijon Noodle) Recipe

Ingredients:

- 1 package rice noodles
- 3 cloves garlic (minced)
- 1 onion (minced)
- 4 cups vegetable stock
- ¼ cup light soy sauce
- 1 teaspoon salt
- ½ teaspoon pepper
- 200 grams flat beans (trimmed)
- 1 large green bell pepper (cut into strips)
- 1 large carrot (cut into strips)
- 200 grams cabbage (shredded)
- 150 grams vegan Que-kiam (kikiam in Filipino)
- 1 tablespoon chopped parsley
- 2 pieces Calamondin (calamansi in Filipino)
- 2 tablespoon vegetable oil

Utensils Needed:

- Wok
- Spatula
- Chopping board
- Kitchen Knife

Directions:

Wash all the vegetables with water. Cut carrots, green bell pepper into strips. Peel garlic husk and onion skin and then mince. Coarsely chop the parsley and cabbage. Cut vegan Que-kiam and calamondin into halves. Trim the flat beans and set all ingredients aside.

Heat 2 tablespoons of vegetable oil in a wok. Add garlic and onion, and then sauté until onion is translucent. Put que-kiam, carrots, cabbage, flat beans, and green bell pepper into the wok and stir-fry until vegetables are tender. Pour 4 cups of vegetable stock and ¼ cup of light soy sauce into the wok. Now, add 1 pack of rice noodles and then bring to simmer. Season with salt and pepper. Add chopped parsley and mix all ingredients well. Serve warm to 6 persons with calamondin on the side.

Health Tips:
- Calamondin or calamansi is a well-known ingredient in Filipino dishes. It's a Filipino lime. It contains a lot of vitamin C, which is beneficial for wound healing and fighting off diseases.

Spicy Taro Leaves with Coconut Milk (Laing)

Ingredients:

- 500 grams dried taro leaves (chopped)
- 5 cups coconut milk
- 2 cups coconut creams
- 7 red chili (minced)
- 2 tablespoon minced ginger
- 3 cloves garlic (minced)
- 1 large onion (sliced)
- 1 tablespoon light soy sauce
- 1 large red chili for garnish
- 2 tablespoon vegetable oil

Utensils Needed:

- Wok
- Ladle
- Chopping board
- Kitchen Knife

Directions:

Rinse dried taro leaves with water and remove the stem. Cut the taro leaves and set aside. Remove the husk of garlic and mince. Wash 7 red chili and cut into small pieces. Mince onion and ginger and save for later use.

Prepare 5 cups of coconut milk and 2 cups of coconut cream. Heat your wok and pour 2 tablespoons of vegetable oil. Add ginger, garlic, onion and red chili into the wok. Sauté until you can smell the spicy aroma of chili. Pour coconut milk and coconut cream into the wok. Bring to simmer. Add 500 grams of taro leaves and season with 1 tablespoon of light soy sauce. Let it boil. When taro leaves wilt, you can easily mix the ingredients using a ladle. Serve with red chili on top to 5 persons.

Health Tips:
- Do you want to have a healthy and glowing skin? Then start eating taro leaves and you look younger than your actual age. Taro contains amino acid that helps produce elastin and collagen. These two substances are the key contributors to having a youthful skin.

Boiled Mix Vegetables (Bulanglang)

Ingredients:

- 5 cups of rice stock/wash
- 200 grams squash (diced)
- 200 grams lady's fingers (cut into halves)
- 200 grams Long beans (cut into 2 inches long)
- 200 grams water spinach
- 2 inches ginger (sliced)
- 200 grams mushroom (cut into halves)
- 200 grams carrots (diced)
- 1 tablespoon light soy sauce
- Salt to taste
- 3 cloves garlic (minced)

Utensils Needed:

- Pot
- Ladle
- Chopping board
- Kitchen knife

Directions:

Prepare all the vegetables and clean with water. Cut each vegetable into desired shapes using a kitchen knife and a chopping board. Set them aside.

Turn on your stove to medium flame. Place a pot of 5 cups rice wash. Add carrots, mushrooms, lady's fingers, squash, long beans, water spinach, ginger, and garlic. Cover the pot and bring to a boil. Add a tablespoon of light soy sauce and sprinkle with salt. Mix using a ladle and cook until vegetables are tender. Serve hot to 4-5 persons.

Health Tips:
- Lady's finger is great for diabetics. You can simply remove the end and place in a glass of water. Soak overnight, and then discard the lady's finger. The sticky liquid from lady's finger helps reduce the sugar level in the body.

Stir-Fried Pumpkin with Long Beans

Ingredients:

- 400 grams pumpkin (cubed)
- 400 grams long beans (cut into 2 inches long)
- 2 medium size tomatoes (diced)
- 2 cloves garlic (minced)
- 3 tablespoon vegetable oil
- 2 tablespoon light soy sauce
- 1 teaspoon salt
- 1 teaspoon pepper

Utensils Needed:

- Wok
- Spatula
- Kitchen Knife
- Chopping board

Directions:

Wash long beans and pumpkin with water. Pat to dry. Peel the pumpkin skin and cut into cubes. Cut the long beans in 2 inches long. Rinse tomatoes, and garlic with water. Mince the garlic and dice the tomatoes. Set them aside.

In a wok with 3 tablespoons of vegetable oil, sauté garlic and tomatoes. Add long beans and stir-fry until it wilt. Put diced pumpkin and cook until tender. Pour 2 tablespoon of light soy sauce and a teaspoon of salt. Sprinkle with pepper. Toss all the ingredients well. Serve warm to 4 persons.

Health Tips:

- Pumpkin is a rich source of Vitamin A. If you don't want to suffer from retinal or vision problem in the future, you should be eating more pumpkins.
- Pumpkin seeds, on the other hand, promotes good sleep. It contains tryptophan, which helps you feel better and relaxed.

Coconut Pandan Vegan Dessert

Ingredients:

- 500 grams shredded coconut
- ¼ cup coconut juice
- 1 cup sweetened coconut milk
- ¾ cup coconut cream
- 1 cup coconut gel
- 2 Pandan leaves
- 100 grams gelatin
- 1 ½ cup water
- ½ cup cooked tapioca pearls

Utensils Needed:

- Saucepan
- Ladle
- Strainer
- Mold
- Kitchen knife
- Large mixing bowl
- Spoon

Directions:

In a large mixing bowl, combine shredded coconut, coconut juice, cooked tapioca pearls and coconut gel. Add 1 cup of coconut milk and ½ cup of coconut cream. Mix all the ingredients well. Put inside the refrigerator.

Get a saucepan and put 1 and ½ cup of water. Add 2 Pandan leaves. Cover the saucepan and bring to boil. Discard the Pandan leaves using a strainer. Pour 100 grams of gelatin into the saucepan and continuously stir until cook. Transfer immediately to a mold. Let it cool and put inside a refrigerator. Cut into cubes once cooled. Add into the mixture of shredded coconut. Combine all ingredients well. Serve chilled to 2 persons.

Health Tips:
- Tapioca helps in blood circulation. It is loaded with iron, a compound that aids in the formation of red blood cells. Without it, blood circulation is impeded in the body.

Seaweed Salad

Ingredients:

- 500 grams fresh seaweed (lato)
- 2 medium size onions (diced)
- 2 medium size tomatoes (cubed)
- 2 tablespoon white vinegar
- 2 tablespoon lime or calamondi extract
- 1 teaspoon white sugar
- Salt and pepper to taste

Utensils Needed:

- Large mixing bowl
- Spoon

Directions:

Rinse 500 grams of fresh seaweeds. Refrigerate until cold. Wash onions and tomatoes with water. Peel the onion and cut into bite size pieces. Chop tomatoes into cubes.

In a large mixing bowl, combine 2 tablespoons of white vinegar and 2 tablespoons of lime extract. Dissolve a teaspoon of sugar into the bowl and season with salt and pepper. Mix thoroughly. Add 500 grams of chilled seaweed and cubed onions and tomatoes. Toss all ingredients and serve to 2 persons.

Health Tips:

- Seaweed contains Calcium that keeps your bone ant teeth strong and healthy. Without adequate amount of calcium intake, you are prone to have bone disease and tooth cavities.

Fresh Spring Rolls

Ingredients:

- 10-12 pieces fresh lettuce leaves
- 250 grams carrots (cut into strips)
- 250 grams jicama (cut into strips)
- 250 grams green bell pepper (cut into strips)
- 250 grams cabbage (shredded)
- 3 garlic cloves (minced)
- 1 large onion (minced)
- 2 tablespoon olive oil
- ½ cup crushed peanuts
- 10-12 pieces vegan rice wrappers
- 2 tablespoon light soy sauce
- 4 tablespoon brown sugar
- 2 cups water
- 4 tablespoon cornstarch

Utensils Needed:

- Wok
- Saucepan
- Mixing bowl
- Spoon
- Spatula
- Ladle
- Mortar and Pestle

Directions:

Prepare all vegetable ingredients. Wash thoroughly with water all the vegetables. Cut carrots, jicama, green bell pepper into strips. Coarsely chop the cabbage into small pieces. Mince onion and garlic. Crush the peanuts using a mortar and pestle.

In a wok, heat 2 tablespoons of vegetable oil. Sauté garlic and onion. When garlic turns brown, add carrots, jicama, green bell pepper, and cabbage. Cook for about 1-2 minutes only. Turn off your stove and set the vegetables aside.

In a saucepan, add 1 cup of water and 4 tablespoons of cornstarch. Mix until cornstarch completely dissolves in the water. Turn on your stove into medium flame. Place the saucepan on the stove. Add another cup of water. Cover the saucepan and bring to boil. Add light soy sauce and brown sugar. Whisk using a ladle. When the mixture thickens, turn off your stove. Set sauce aside.

Get your vegan rice wrappers. Place 1 piece of lettuce leaf on the wrapper. Add the mixed vegetables in the center of the lettuce. Wet all sides of the wrapper with water. Fold it and secure at the center. Pour Sauce on top of the wrapper and sprinkle with crushed peanuts. Do the same with the remaining wrappers. Serve chilled to 5-6 persons.

Health Tips:
- Lettuce contains folate, which is essential for the healthy metabolism of DNA in the body. This is especially good for pregnant women since it prevents neural tube defects in an unborn child.
- Jicama is a good source of Vitamin C. Vitamin C helps the body to fight against infection and prevents cancer cells.

Fried Eggplant with Spicy Sauce

Ingredients:

- 7 pieces Eggplant
- 4 tablespoon vegetable oil
- 7 tablespoon tamari sauce
- 5 pieces red chili)chopped)
- 1 onion (minced)
- 1 tablespoon white vinegar

Utensils Needed:

- Wok
- Spatula
- Kitchen knife
- Chopping board
- Mixing bowl
- Spoon

Directions:

Rinse 7 pieces eggplant with cold running water. Pat to dry. Cut into halves, and then chop into 2 inches long. Wash onion and red chili. Remove the onion skin and mince. Chop red chili into small pieces and set aside.

In a mixing bowl, pour 7 tablespoons of tamari sauce. Add a tablespoon of white vinegar and mix in minced onions and red chili. Whisk using a spoon until mixture combine.

Heat 4 tablespoons of vegetable oil in a wok. When oil shimmers, chopped eggplants. Stir-fry until eggplants wilt. Some like it crispy. It depends on your preference. Serve hot to 4-5 persons with spicy sauce.

Health Tips:
- When preparing an eggplant dish, it's always better to include the eggplant skin. The skin contains a lot of Nasunin, a phytonutrient compound that fights against free radical damage. This means you prevent yourself from getting cancer.

Jackfruit in Coconut Milk

Ingredients:

- 500 grams unripe Jackfruit (diced)
- 1 large onion (sliced)
- 3 cloves garlic (minced)
- 2 inches ginger (minced)
- 5 pieces green chili
- 1 piece chopped green chili for garnish
- 2 cups coconut milk
- 1 cup coconut cream
- 2 tablespoon light soy sauce
- 2 teaspoon salt
- 1 teaspoon pepper
- ½ cup water

Utensils Needed:

- Pot
- Ladle
- Kitchen knife
- Chopping board

Directions:

Prepare 500 grams of unripe jackfruit. Cut into cubes. Wash green chili, onion, ginger and garlic with water. Peel onion, garlic, and ginger. Mince them all and then set aside. Save 1 pieces of chopped green chili for garnish.

Turn on your stove to medium heat. Put the pot on the stove. Pour 2 cups of coconut milk, 1 cup of coconut cream and ½ cup of water into the pot. Add 500 grams of unripe jackfruit. Mix in minced garlic, ginger, onion and green chili. Cover the pot and cook until jackfruit is soft. Stir occasionally to avoid burning. When sauce thickens, add light soy sauce, salt, and pepper. Cover the pot and bring to simmer. Garnish with chopped green chili and serve hot to 5 persons.

Health Tips:
- Jackfruit has a lot of fiber that aids in good digestion. It also removes toxins in the colon and prevents you from getting colon cancer.

Eggplant Salad

Ingredients:

- 3 large Eggplants
- 2 medium size onions (chopped)
- 2 medium size tomatoes (diced)
- 2 tablespoon white vinegar
- 1 tablespoon Calamondin (Calamansi) extract
- 1 tablespoon white sugar
- 2 teaspoon salt
- 1 teaspoon pepper

Utensils Needed:

- Broiler
- Aluminum foil
- Baking pan
- Fork
- Mixing bowl

Directions:

Wash 3 eggplants with water and then pat to dry. Cover each eggplant with aluminum foil. Place on a baking pan. Save for later use. Cut onions and tomatoes into cubes and set aside.

Preheat your broiler and cook the eggplant for 25 minutes. Once the eggplant is scorched, you can turn off your broiler. Let eggplants cool in room temperature> remove the eggplant skin and transfer the cooked eggplant in a mixing bowl. Mash the eggplant using a fork. Add chopped onions and tomatoes into the mixing bowl. Pour 2 tablespoons of white vinegar into the bowl. Squeeze Calamondin extract to the bowl and then whisk all ingredients well. Season with salt and pepper. Serve chilled to 4 persons.

Health Tips:
- Tomatoes help lowers bad cholesterol level in the body. This means fat accumulation in your blood vessels is reduced. This keeps your cardiovascular system healthy and strong.

Water Spinach Adobo (cooked in vinegar, soy sauce and garlic)

Ingredients:

- 400 grams of water spinach (chopped)
- 8 garlic cloves (chopped)
- ½ cup soy sauce (use tamari sauce)
- ¼ cup white vinegar
- 2 tablespoon vegetable oil
- 1 teaspoon salt
- ½ teaspoon pepper

Utensils Needed:

- Frying pan
- Spatula
- Kitchen knife
- Chopping board

Directions:

Thoroughly wash water spinach with water. Remove the end part of the stem and dried or yellowish leaves. Chop the water spinach and set aside. Peel the garlic skin and chop the garlic.

In a frying pan over medium heat, add 2 tablespoons of vegetable oil. When oil is hot and shimmering, add the chopped garlic. Stir-fry until garlic turns brown. Pour tamari sauce and vinegar and then bring to simmer. Add 400 grams of water spinach and cook until the stem is tender. Season with salt and pepper. Toss all ingredients together and then serve warm to 4 persons.

Health Tips:
- Eating water spinach can prevent you from acquiring anemia or blood-related problems. It contains Iron that helps increase hemoglobin level in the body.

Creamy Coconut Papaya with Horseradish Leaves

Ingredients:

- 500 grams unripe papaya (sliced)
- 1 cup horseradish leaves
- 2 cups coconut milk
- 1 cup coconut cream
- ½ cup water
- 2 tablespoon light soy sauce
- 4 pieces red chili (chopped)
- 3 inches ginger (minced)
- 3 cloves garlic (minced)
- 1 large onion (chopped)
- Salt and pepper to taste

Utensils Needed:

- Saucepan
- Ladle
- Kitchen knife
- Chopping board

Directions:

Wash unripe papaya with water and then peel the skin. Cut diagonally into 2 inches long. Wash onions, garlic, ginger and red chili with water and then chop into small pieces. Rinse horseradish leaves and then trim. Set aside.

In a saucepan, pour 2 cups of coconut milk, ½ cup of water and 1 cup of coconut cream. Turn your stove to medium flame and cover the pot. Bring to simmer and then add ginger, red chili, onions and garlic. Mix ingredients using a ladle. Now, add papaya and horseradish leaves. Cook until papaya is tender. Pour 2 tablespoons of light soy sauce and season with salt and pepper. Stir occasionally. Once sauce thickens, you can serve it to 4 persons with rice.

Health Tips:
- Papaya can treat inflammation caused by arthritis, asthma and even burns. The enzyme papain and chemopapain found in papaya reduces inflammation and improves healing.

Garlic Fried Rice

Ingredients:

- 3 cups cooked rice
- 8 cloves garlic (minced)
- A bunch of spring onions (chopped)
- 3 tablespoon of vegetable oil
- 1 tablespoon of light soy sauce
- 1 teaspoon salt
- 1 teaspoon pepper

Utensils Needed:

- Wok
- Spatula
- Chopping board
- Kitchen knife

Directions:

Prepare 3 cups of cooked rice, 8 cloves garlic and a bunch of spring onions. Wash spring onions and garlic with water. Chop the spring onions into small pieces, save 1 tablespoon for garnish. Mince the garlic.

Heat 3 tablespoons of vegetable oil in a wok. Sauté garlic until it turns brown. Slowly mix in cooked rice into the wok to avoid clumping of rice. When you're done adding all 3 cups of rice, add the chopped spring onions. Continuously stir all ingredients. Pour 1 tablespoon of light soy sauce and sprinkle salt and pepper. Mix well until rice is completely coated.

Garnish with spring onions and serve hot to 5-6 persons.

Health Tips:
- According to some research, garlic is as potent as cardiovascular medications to treat hypertension. Garlic lowers your blood pressure and prevents you from getting a heart attack.

Caramelized Sweet Potatoes

Ingredients:

- 500 grams sweet potatoes (sliced)
- ½ cup white sugar
- ½ cup brown sugar
- Vegetable oil for deep frying

Utensils Needed:

- Kitchen knife
- Wok
- Chopping board
- Spatula
- Strainer
- Skewer

Directions:

Remove dirt from sweet potatoes by rinsing it with running water. Peel the skin and then cut into your desired shape.

Heat about 2 cups of vegetable oil in a wok over medium flame. When oil is shimmering and hot. Pour ½ cup of brown sugar. Cook until sugar melts and then add 500 grams of chopped sweet potatoes. Carefully mix in the melted sugar and sweet potatoes together. Add another half cup of brown sugar and let it melt. Once sweet potatoes are crispy, strain excess oil. You can skewer the sweet potatoes on a bamboo stick or you can serve it on a plate. Serve warm to 5-6 persons.

Health Tips:

- Sweet potatoes have beta-carotene and vitamin C, which enhances your immune system. A healthy and strong immune system can prevent you from acquiring different diseases.

Squash with Bitter Melon Leaves Soup

Ingredients:

- 400 grams squash (cubed)
- 300 grams bitter melon leaves
- 3 cups vegetable broth
- 2 cups water
- 1 teaspoon salt
- ½ teaspoon pepper
- 2 cloves garlic (chopped)
- 1 medium size onion (sliced)

Utensils Needed:

- Pot
- Ladle
- Chopping board
- Kitchen knife

Directions:

Peel the skin of squash after washing with water and then cut into cubes. Rinse bitter melon leaves and remove any yellowish or dried leaves. Chop both onions and garlic.

Boil 2 cups of water in a pot. Add garlic and onion. Stir using a ladle and then pour 3 cups of vegetable broth. Now, add 400 grams of cubed squash and 300 grams of bitter melon leaves. Cover the pot and let it simmer. Sprinkle with salt and pepper. Mix occasionally. Cook until squash is tender. Serve hot to 5 persons.

Health Tips:

- Bitter melon leaves have many medicinal benefits. It can treat intestinal parasite, diabetes, asthma, arthritis and even cholera. Drinking juice out of bitter melon leaves can give your body phytochemicals, which prevents you from getting different forms of illnesses.

Fruit Salad Filipino Style

Ingredients:

- 2 cups coconut milk
- 1 cup coconut cream
- ½ cup sugar
- 2 cans of fruit cocktail
- 1 can nata de coco
- 1 cup diced apple
- ¼ cup cherry (cut into halves)

Utensils Needed:

- Large mixing bowl
- 2 big wooden spoon
- Colander
- Blender
- Kitchen knife
- Chopping board

Directions:

Prepare 2 cans of fruit cocktail. Using a colander, drain the liquid and discard. Transfer mixed fruits in a large mixing bowl. Set aside.

Wash apples and peel the skin, and then cut into cubes. Rinse cherries and cut into halves. Open 1 can of nata de coco and drain syrup using a colander. Now, get the prepared mixed fruits and add the cubed apples, cherries and nata de coco. Save for later use.

Get a blender and pour 2 cups of coconut milk. Add 1 cup of coconut cream and ½ cup of white sugar. Blend until mixture thickens. Pour coconut mixture into the bowl of mixed fruits. Carefully toss all the ingredients together using two wooden spoons. Cover the bowl and refrigerate overnight. Serve chilled to 6 persons.

Health Tips:
- Apples are rich in fiber and are good for cleansing the teeth and gums. If you want a natural way of cleaning your teeth after a meal, then you should eat some apples.

Vermicelli Noodle (Misua) with Sponge Gourd

Ingredients:

- 100 grams vermicelli noodle (Misua)
- 2 cups of water
- 1 cup vegetable stock
- 3 pieces Sponge gourd (cut thinly)
- 3 inches ginger (minced)
- 5 cloves garlic (minced)
- Salt and pepper to taste
- 1 tablespoon light soy sauce
- 1 large onion (minced)

Utensils Needed:

- Pot
- Ladle
- Kitchen knife
- Chopping board

Directions:

Prepare onions, ginger and garlic. Rinse with water and remove the skin. Mince and set them aside. Wash sponge gourd and slice thinly.

Boil 2 cups of water in a pot over medium heat. Now, add sliced sponge gourd, minced garlic, ginger and onion into the pot. Mix using a ladle. Cover the pot and bring to simmer. Once sponge gourd is tender, add 100 grams of vermicelli noodles (Misua). Pour 1 cup of vegetable stock and let it boil. Mix in a tablespoon of light soy sauce and sprinkle with salt and pepper. Cook until vermicelli noodles are soft. Stir occasionally. Serve hot to 6 persons.

Health Tips:
- Are you experiencing muscle pain or spasm? You might be lacking the compound Potassium in your body. Potassium is an essential electrolyte to help balance fluids inside the body and prevents muscle pain and cramps. Sponge gourd contains ample amount of potassium that can prevent muscle pain and spasm.

Sautéed Cabbage with Mushroom

Ingredients:

- 350 grams mushroom (julienned)
- 1 head cabbage (sliced thinly)
- 2 tablespoon vegetable oil
- 1 tablespoon tamari sauce
- 1 teaspoon salt
- ½ teaspoon pepper
- ½ cup vegetable broth
- 1 large tomato (cut into strips)
- 1 large onion (sliced)
- 2 cloves garlic (minced)

Utensils Needed:

- Frying pan
- Spatula
- Kitchen knife
- Chopping board

Directions:

Wash all vegetables with cold running water. Be sure to remove any dirt from the cabbage. Cut cabbage, tomatoes, onions, and mushroom into thin strips. Mince the garlic.

Now, heat 2 tablespoons of vegetable oil in a wok. Once the oil is hot, sauté garlic, onions, and tomatoes. Add 350 grams of mushroom and stir-fry until mushroom is tender. Pour ½ cup of vegetable stock into the wok and let it simmer. Then, add the shredded cabbage and mix all the ingredients well. Season with a tablespoon of tamari sauce and sprinkle with salt and pepper. Continuously stir all ingredients to avoid burning the vegetables. Cook for about 5 minutes and then serve to 6 persons.

Health Tips:
- Do you want to stay focused and become smarter? Cabbage is one of the healthiest vegetables for the brain. It contains Anthocyanins and vitamin K, which helps your brain cells become more active. Eating cabbage improves your overall cognitive function.

Tofu in Thick Tomato Sauce

Ingredients:

- 450 grams tofu (cubed)
- 10 pieces large tomatoes (diced)
- ¼ cup vegetable broth
- 2 cloves garlic (minced)
- Salt and pepper to taste
- 3 tablespoon vegetable oil
- 1 large onion (minced)

Utensils Needed:

- Frying pan
- Spatula
- Kitchen Knife
- Fork
- Mixing bowl
- Chopping board

Directions:

Rinse and drain 450 grams of tofu and then cut into cubes. Wash tomatoes, onions and garlic. After washing, remove the garlic husk and onion skin. Mince both garlic and onion. Then, dice 10 pieces of tomatoes and place in a mixing bowl. Mash the tomatoes using a fork and save for later use.

In a frying pan, pour 3 tablespoons of vegetable oil. Once the oil is hot, sauté garlic and onion. Add cubed tofu and stir-fry until golden on both sides. Now, put the mashed tomatoes into the frying pan and add ¼ cup of vegetable broth. Stir frequently and allow the sauce to thicken. Serve warm to 5-6 persons.

Health Tips:

- Tofu is a good non-dairy source of Calcium that keeps your bone healthy and strong. It also contains other minerals that can improve your bone health like Phosphorus and Manganese.

Mixed Vegetables in Tamarind Soup

Ingredients:

- 3 cups of water
- 2 cups of vegetable stock
- 1 cup tamarind extract or concentrate
- 1 medium size eggplant (chopped)
- 5 pieces lady's finger (sliced)
- 2 bunch of water spinach (chopped)
- 2 large tomatoes (sliced)
- 1 large onion (chopped)
- 1 large daikon (cut thinly)
- Salt and pepper to taste

Utensils Needed:

- Pot
- Ladle
- Chopping board
- Knife

Directions:

Gather all ingredients. Wash all vegetables with water. Peel the onions and daikon. Chop each vegetable into your desired shape. Set them aside for later use.

Turn your stove into medium heat. Place a pot on top of the stove and pour 3 cups of water into the pot. Add onions and tomatoes and let it boil. Add each vegetable one at a time, starting with eggplant, then lady's finger, followed by daikon and water spinach. Pour 2 cups of vegetable broth into the pot and add 1 cup of tamarind extract. Stir all ingredients and cover the pot. Cook until vegetables are tender. Season with salt and pepper. Constantly stir the soup while cooking. Serve hot to 6 persons.

Health Tips:

◦ Eating daikon can help your kidneys excrete all toxins out of your body. Daikon is a potent vegetable diuretic, which increases your urination. Elimination of waste product through frequent urination keeps your body healthy.

◦ Tamarind has HCA (Hydroxycitric Acid), a substance that prevents storage of fats into your body. It works in blocking a specific enzyme that regulates fat absorption. This means, eating tamarind or adding tamarind in your meals will help you lose weight.

Creamy Macaroni Pasta Soup with Mixed Vegetables

Ingredients:

- 500 grams macaroni pasta
- 2 cups water
- 1 cup vegetable broth
- 1 cup coconut milk or almond milk
- 1 cup coconut cream
- 1 large carrot (julienned)
- 1 bunch spring onion (chopped)
- ½ head cabbage (shredded)
- 4 cloves garlic (minced)
- 1 large onion (chopped)
- 2 tablespoon vegetable oil
- Salt and pepper to taste

Utensils Needed:

- Pot
- Ladle
- Kitchen knife
- Chopping board

Directions:

    Rinse carrots, onions, garlic, cabbage and spring onion with cold water. Cut carrots and cabbage into thin strips, and mince both garlic and onions. Chop spring onions and save 1 tablespoon for garnish.

    Heat 2 tablespoons of vegetable oil in a pot, and then sauté garlic and onion. Once onion turns translucent, pour 2 cups of water, 1 cup of vegetable broth, and a cup of coconut milk into the pot. Cover the pot and bring to boil. Now, add

400 grams of macaroni pasta. Cook pasta until al dente and then add a cup of coconut cream. Put carrots, cabbage, and spring onions into the pot. Cover the pot after mixing all the ingredients. Let it simmer, then season with salt and pepper. Cook for about 5 minutes until pasta is soft. Serve hot to 6 persons.

Health Tips:

- Pasta is vegan-friendly. There are many varieties of pasta like macaroni pasta. A whole-wheat macaroni is equipped with Iron that is essential in hemoglobin production in your body. Without hemoglobin, no organ in your body would get enough supply of oxygen and this could lead to organ failure.

Vegetable Curry Filipino Style

Ingredients:

- 2 large potatoes (diced)
- 1 large carrot (cubed)
- 1 bay leaf
- 2 teaspoon curry powder
- ½ cup water
- 1 cup coconut milk
- 1 large green bell pepper
- 200 grams green peas
- Salt and pepper to taste
- 250 grams mushroom
- 200 grams pineapple chunks
- 3 garlic cloves (minced)

Utensils Needed:

- Saucepan
- Ladle
- Kitchen knife
- Chopping board
- Strainer
- Bowl

Directions:

Wash potatoes, green bell pepper, and garlic, carrots, mushroom and green peas with water. For green peas, place in a bowl and discard any floating green peas. Mince the garlic and cut all vegetables into cubes. Open a can of pineapple chunks and drain the syrup using a strainer. Save for later use.

In a saucepan, pour ½ cup of water and 1 cup of coconut milk. Add minced garlic, cubed potatoes, carrots, green bell pepper, and mushroom. Cover the saucepan and bring to boil. Cook until potatoes are tender. Now, add green peas and pineapple chunks. Add 2 teaspoons of curry powder and then put 1 bay leaf into the saucepan. Let it simmer and sprinkle with salt and pepper. Stir occasionally until sauce thickens. Serve warm with rice to 5 persons.

Health Tips:

- Bay leaf has an antibacterial function in treating kidney infections. It can also help remove kidney stones. Including bay leaf in your recipe will help you maintain a normal kidney function.

Rice Purple Yam Cake in Bamboo Tube (Puto Bumbong)

Ingredients:

- 500 grams glutinous rice flour
- 250 grams purple yam powder
- 3 cups water
- Muscovado sugar for garnish
- Grated coconut for garnish

Utensils Needed:

- Steamer
- Bamboo tube
- Large mixing bowl
- Banana leaf
- Wooden spoon

Directions:

Combine glutinous rice flour and purple yam powder in a large mixing bowl. Slowly add 3 cups of water into the bowl while mixing. When the mixture turns to a dough, knead it until stiff.

Prepare bamboo tubes. Transfer the dough into bamboo tubes and attach it to a steamer. Steam until mist comes out of the bamboo tubes. Make sure to tap the bamboo tubes occasionally when steaming to make sure the dough cooks evenly. Place cooked dough on a banana leaf and sprinkle with Muscovado sugar and grated coconut. Serve to 5-6 persons.

Health Tips:

- Muscovado sugar is a type of brown sugar. It's refined and natural cane sugar. It contains molasses that give Muscovado its brown color. Natural cane sugar like Muscovado is richer in minerals compared to normal white sugar. It has more potassium, calcium, and iron, meaning it's healthier compared to white sugar. Adding Muscovado sugar in your recipe doesn't only give color but is also better for your health.

Spicy and Hot Garlic Beans with Coconut Milk

Ingredients:

- 500 grams green beans (baguio beans) chopped
- 4 pieces red chili (chopped)
- 7 cloves garlic (minced)
- 1 cup coconut milk
- 1 cup coconut cream
- 1 large onion (minced)
- 2 teaspoon salt
- 1 tablespoon light soy sauce
- 1 teaspoon ground black pepper
- 2 tablespoon vegetable oil

Utensils Needed:

- Saucepan
- Spatula
- Kitchen knife
- Chopping board

Directions:

Prepare 500 grams of green beans. Wash with cold water and trim. Chop into small pieces and set aside. Rinse garlic, red chili and onion with water. Then, mince garlic and onion. Slice red chili into small sizes and leave 1 whole red chili for garnish.

Heat 2 tablespoons of vegetable oil in a saucepan. Sauté

garlic and onion until onion turns transparent. Add chopped green beans and stir-fry until tender. Pour a cup of coconut milk and coconut cream into the saucepan. Mix in the chopped red chili and cover the saucepan. Let it boil and allow the sauce to thicken. Occasionally stir to cook all ingredients evenly. Add a tablespoon of light soy sauce and season with salt and pepper. Mix well and bring to simmer. Serve hot with rice to 5 persons.

Health Tips:

- Pepper is good for digestion and prevents you from having stomachache, constipation or diarrhea. It can also treat ulcers according to some recent studies. The anti-inflammatory properties of pepper keeps your gastric linings from damage due to high acidic environment in your stomach.

Radish Salad Filipino Style

Ingredients:

- 3 pieces radish (sliced)
- 1/4 cup white cane vinegar
- 1 large onion (chopped)
- 1 large tomato (sliced)
- 1 teaspoon sugar
- 1 tablespoon Calamondin (Calamansi) extract
- 1 tablespoon salt for soaking
- ¼ teaspoon pepper
- 1 teaspoon salt

Utensils Needed:

- Large mixing bowl
- Colander
- Spoon
- Kitchen knife
- Chopping board

Directions:

Wash 3 pieces radish with water and peel the skin. Slice and put in a large mixing bowl. Sprinkle with salt and mix. Set aside for 15-20 minutes then mash and drain in a colander to remove the bitter taste of radish. Wash with cold running water and transfer to a large mixing bowl.

Chop tomatoes and onions and put in the bowl of radish. Pour ¼ cup of white cane vinegar and squeeze about a tablespoon of Calamondin extract into the bowl. Sprinkle with a teaspoon of sugar and season with pepper and salt. Toss all ingredients to mix well. Serve chilled to 6 persons.

Health Tips:
- White cane vinegar comes from sugarcane extract. It has antimicrobial properties that kill bacteria in your body. This is the reason why vinegar is always used for fermentation and preservation of food.

Sautéed Bok Choy (Pechay) in Vinegar, Garlic and Soy Sauce

Ingredients:

- 1 kg Bok Choy (chopped)
- 7 garlic cloves (chopped)
- 1 medium size onion (minced)
- 1 medium size tomato (chopped)
- ½ cup vegetable stock
- 2 tablespoon vegan soy sauce
- 1 tablespoon of vinegar
- 1 teaspoon pepper
- 2 tablespoon vegetable oil

Utensils Needed:

- Wok
- Spatula
- Kitchen knife
- Chopping board

Directions:

Rinse 1 kg of Bok Choy (Pechay) with water and remove yellowish and dried leaves. Cut off the end of Bok Choy stem and chop into small pieces. Wash tomato, onion and garlic and slice into small pieces.

Now, place a wok on top of a stove. Turn stove to medium flame and pour 2 tablespoon of vegetable oil into the wok. Once the oil is hot, sauté garlic, onion and tomato. Stir-fry until garlic becomes brown. Add 1 kg of Bok Choy (Pechay) and ½ cup of vegetable stock into the wok. Bring to simmer.

Frequently toss all ingredients to avoid burning the Bok Choy. Add 2 tablespoon of vegan soy sauce (you may use tamari sauce) and a tablespoon of vinegar. Season with pepper. Cook for about 5 minutes and serve warm with rice to 6 persons.

Health Tips:
- Pechay is a local cabbage variety in the Philippines. It is also known as Bok Choy or green cabbage. Making a dish out of Pechay will help you fight against infection because it contains ample amount of Vitamin C, which is beneficial in boosting your immunity.

Banana Blossoms in Creamy Coconut Sauce

Ingredients:

- Ingredients:
- 1 piece banana blossoms (shredded or julienned)
- 1 cup coconut milk
- ½ cup vegetable broth
- ½ cup coconut cream
- 2 inches ginger (grated)
- 1 medium size onion (chopped)
- 5 cloves garlic (minced)
- 2 tablespoon vegetable oil
- 1 tablespoon vinegar
- Pepper and salt to taste
- 2-3 pieces long banana pepper (cut into 2 inches diagonally)

Utensils Needed:

- Wok
- Spatula
- Kitchen Knife
- Chopping board

Directions:

Get 1 piece of banana blossom. Wash with water and peel off the fibrous outer part. Cut the stem and slice into thin strips the softer inner layer of the banana blossom. Prepare ginger, garlic, banana pepper, and onion. Mince garlic and grate the ginger. Now, chop the onions and banana pepper, and then set aside.

Place 2 tablespoon of vegetable oil in a wok. When oil is shimmering, add garlic, ginger and onion. Sauté until ginger turns brown and onion becomes translucent. Add the shredded banana blossom and pour a cup of coconut milk. Mix in ½ cup of coconut cream and half a cup of vegetable stock. Stir the ingredients and bring to a boil. When the sauce thickens, add vinegar and chopped banana pepper. Stir all ingredients thoroughly. Season with pepper. Cook for another 2 minutes and then serve warm with rice to 6 persons.

Health Tips:
- Banana Blossom is edible for cooking in the Philippines and some other Asian countries. If you want to improve your mood and become more energetic, make sure to eat some banana blossoms. It has Magnesium that can prevent you from being sad and lonely, and helps you to have a lighter and happier mood.

Coconut Corn Pudding (Maja Blanca)

Ingredients:

- 6 cups coconut milk
- 2 cups almond milk
- 1 cup evaporated cane juice
- ¼ cup white cane sugar
- 1 can sweet corn cream style
- 1 cup corn starch
- 1 cup coconut milk (toasted for garnish)

Utensils Needed:

- Pot
- Ladle
- Large baking pan
- Banana leaf
- Wok
- Spatula
- Colander

Directions:

Gather all ingredients, and then turn on your stove to medium heat. Place a pot on top of the stove and then pour 2 cups of almond milk and 6 cups of coconut milk. Mix and cover the pot and then bring to simmer. Add a cup of evaporated cane juice and dissolve a ¼ cup of white cane sugar into the pot. Slowly add 1 cup of cornstarch into the pot while stirring. Continuously mix until cornstarch dissolves into the mixture. Now, add 1 can of sweet corn into the pot and whisk using a ladle. Bring to a simmer then transfer to a large baking pan. Let it cool.

In a wok over medium heat, cook 1 cup of coconut milk. Stir continuously until coconut milk curdles and turns brown. You will notice oil coming out from the coconut milk as it turns brown while cooking. Cook for about 30 minutes while stirring constantly. Remove from heat and strain excess oil using a colander. Sprinkle toasted coconut into the cooled coconut pudding. Refrigerate for a couple of hours or overnight. Cut the coconut pudding into cubes and place on a banana leaf. Serve chilled to 8-10 persons.

Health Tips:
- If you want to maintain a normal blood pressure and have a healthy heart, you should add coconut milk in your meals. Coconut milk contains Lauric acid that lowers blood cholesterol level in the body. This keeps your blood pressure in control and you'll have a lower irks of developing any heart problem.
- Corn is a rich source of fiber, which helps in proper digestion. The high content of fiber in corn also reduces your risk of developing colon or rectal cancer.

Rice Porridge with Tofu

Ingredients:

- 1 cup rice
- 6 cups water
- 1 cup vegetable stock
- 400 grams tofu (cubed)
- 3 inches ginger (grated)
- 6 cloves garlic (minced)
- A bunch of spring onions (chopped)
- 1 large onion (minced)
- 3 tablespoon of vegetable oil
- 1 teaspoon pepper
- 1 teaspoon salt
- 1 tablespoon light soy sauce

Utensils Needed:

- Pot
- Ladle
- Wok
- Spatula
- Kitchen knife
- Chopping board

Directions:

Rinse and drain 400 grams of tofu. Cut into cubes. Heat 2 tablespoons of vegetable oil in a wok, then stir-fry cubed tofu until golden on both sides. Save for later use.

Prepare onion, ginger and garlic. Wash with water and cut into small pieces. Now, heat a tablespoon of vegetable oil in a pot over medium flame. Sauté garlic until brown. Add ginger and onion and stir-fry until onion becomes transparent. Pour 6 cups of water and a cup of vegetable stock into the pot. Add 1 cup of uncooked rice. Stir to combine ingredients and then cover the pot. Bring to a boil and reduce the stove to lower the heat. Whisk occasionally to avoid burning the rice. When the porridge becomes thick, sprinkle it with chopped spring onions, salt and pepper and a tablespoon of light soy sauce. Add the fried tofu and carefully combine all ingredients. Cook for another 5-7 minutes, while stirring constantly. Serve warm to 4-5 persons.

Health Tips:
- If your pregnant and is suffering from morning sickness like nausea. Ginger is your best natural treatment. According to many studies, ginger is a very effective remedy to relieve nausea among pregnant women. It can also help relieve nausea caused by chemotherapy and nausea symptoms of post-surgical patients.

Bitter Gourd Salad Filipino Style

Ingredients:

- 2 bitter gourd (cut thinly)
- 2 medium size onions (julienned)
- 2 medium size tomatoes (diced)
- ¼ cup vinegar
- 2 tablespoon lemon extract
- 1 tablespoon honey
- 1 teaspoon pepper
- 2 tablespoon salt
- 2 cups water

Utensils Needed:

- Large mixing bowl
- Colander
- Wooden spoon
- Plastic wrap
- Chopping board
- Kitchen knife

Directions:

Wash 2 pieces of bitter gourd, tomatoes, and onions. Peel tomatoes and cut into thin strips. Dice the tomatoes and then cut the bitter gourd into halves. Remove the seeds and slice into strips.

Place strips of bitter gourd in a large mixing bowl and then add 2 tablespoons of salt. Thoroughly rub the bitter gourd with salt, then pour 2 cups of water into the bowl. Soak for about an hour and then drain the water using a colander.

Now, add diced tomatoes and onion strips into the bowl. Add ¼ cup of vinegar and 2 tablespoons of lemon extract. Slowly add a tablespoon of honey while tossing all the ingredients using a fork. Season with pepper and mix well. Cover the bowl with a plastic wrap and refrigerate for a couple of hours. Serve chilled to 6 persons.

Health Tips:
- Adding pure lemon extract in your dish can prevent you from having kidney stones. It can also help treat urinary tract infections. The antimicrobial property of lemon extract helps fight infection and bacteria.

Coleslaw Filipino Style

Ingredients:

- 1 head cabbage (shredded)
- 1 medium size carrot (julienned)
- 1 medium size onion (cut into thin strips)
- ½ cup virgin olive oil
- 1 teaspoon apple cider vinegar
- ¼ cup soy milk (unsweetened)
- Salt to taste
- Pepper to taste

Utensils Needed:

- Blender
- Kitchen knife
- Chopping board
- Wooden spoon
- Mixing bowl

Directions:

Wash cabbage with water and cut into strips. Peel 1 medium size carrot and 1 medium size onion, then slice into thin strips. Place in a large mixing bowl and set aside.

To make a salad dressing, prepare soymilk, apple cider vinegar, salt to taste and olive oil. Get a blender and combine all the ingredients together. Blend until mixture consistency becomes smooth.

Put salad dressing in the bowl of mixed cabbage and carrots. Toss all ingredients using a wooden spoon. Sprinkle with pepper and refrigerate for a couple of hours. Serve chilled to 3-4 persons.

Health Tips:
- Apple cider vinegar has been proven beneficial to diabetics. It maintains a normal the blood glucose level in the body. Drinking a glass of water mixed with a tablespoon of apple cider once before bedtime balances blood sugar level in the body upon waking up.

Cassava with Grated Coconut Dessert

Ingredients:

- 2 cups cassava (grated)
- 1 cup coconut milk
- 1 cup water
- 1 cup white cane sugar
- 1 teaspoon lye water
- 2 teaspoon Pandan essence
- 1 cup coconut (grated)

Utensils Needed:

- Steamer
- Small molds
- Large mixing bowl
- Metal whisker
- Baking sheet
- Shredder
- Peeler

Directions:

Peel cassava and wash with cold running water. Pat to dry. Using a shredder, grate the cassava. Combine grated cassava, a cup of water, and a cup of coconut milk in a large mixing bowl. Dissolve 1 cup of white cane sugar and add 2 teaspoon of Pandan essence. Mix the mixture until smooth. Gradually pour 1 teaspoon of lye water into the mixture while whisking.

Prepare small molds and pour cassava mixture into each molds. Cook on a steamer over medium flame. Steam for about an hour or until cassava turns translucent. Remove the molds from the steamer and let it cool for about 15 minutes.

Refrigerate the cassava for 3-4 hours and then remove cassava from the mold.

In a baking sheet, sprinkle a cup of grated coconut. Roll each cassava on the grated coconut and then transfer to a plate. Serve chilled to 4-5 persons.

Health Tips:
- Cassava is a great source of protein. It is a good alternative protein source for vegans. Protein is important in building and repairing body tissues. Making dishes out of cassava will surely boosts your body's ability of repairing itself.

Asparagus Soup Filipino Style

Ingredients:

- A bunch of Asparagus (trimmed and chopped)
- 1 cup of coconut milk
- 2 teaspoon of garlic powder
- 2 teaspoon of ginger (grated)
- 2 cups of vegetable stock
- 1 cup coconut cream
- Salt and pepper to taste
- 1 onion (minced)
- 2 tablespoon vegetable oil

Utensils Needed:

- Pot
- Ladle
- Chopping board
- Kitchen knife
- Shredder

Directions:

Wash and trim a bunch of asparagus, then cut into 2 inches long. Rinse onion, and ginger with water and then peel the skin. Mince the onion and using a shredder, grate the ginger. Save for later use.

Put 2 tablespoons of vegetable oil in a pot. Heat over medium flame. Sauté ginger and onions. Add asparagus and stir-fry until tender. Pour a cup of coconut milk, a cup of coconut cream and 2 cups of vegetable stock into the pot. Whisk using a ladle and cover the pot. Bring to a boil and then add garlic powder. Make sure to stir occasionally while cooking. Allow the soup to thicken and then sprinkle with salt and pepper. Mix well. Serve hot to 5-6 persons.

Health Tips:
- If you want to increase your cognitive abilities, you should eat food rich in folate and vitamin B12. One good example of a vegetable rich in this vitamins is asparagus. It can boost your brain cells ability and improve your overall cognitive performance.

Sweet and Sour Tofu with Mixed Vegetables

Ingredients:

- 500 grams tofu (diced)
- 1 large red bell pepper (cubed)
- 1 large green bell pepper (cubed)
- 200 grams mushroom (sliced)
- 1 cup pineapple chunks
- 2 tablespoon ketchup
- 2 tablespoon white vinegar
- 1 tablespoon lemon extract
- 2 tablespoon light soy sauce
- 2 teaspoon corn starch mixed with 2 tablespoon water
- 3 tablespoon white cane sugar
- ½ cup water
- 2 tablespoon vegetable oil
- 2 teaspoon garlic powder

Utensils Needed:

- Saucepan
- Spatula
- Kitchen knife
- Chopping board

Directions:

Prepare green bell pepper, red bell pepper, and mushroom. Wash with water and cut pepper into cubes, while cut mushrooms into halves. Rinse and drain tofu, then chop into small blocks.

Place a saucepan on a stove and turn on medium flame. Heat 2 tablespoons of vegetable oil and then add cubed tofu. Stir-fry until brown on both sides. Add green bell pepper, red bell pepper, and mushrooms into the saucepan. Cook until vegetables become tender. Now, pour 2 tablespoons of ketchup and white vinegar. Add the cornstarch mixture and 2 tablespoons of light soy sauce. Stir to combine all ingredients. Add a tablespoon of lemon extract and pour ½ cup of water. Cover the saucepan and let it simmer. When the sauce thickens, season with 2 teaspoons of garlic powder. Cook for another 1-2 minutes while stirring occasionally. Serve warm with rice to 4-5 persons.

Health Tips:

- If you're having cough episodes and you can go out of your house to buy cough medicines, then just eat some pineapples and your cough will surely go away. Pineapple contains a compound called Bromelain. It removes phlegm out of your respiratory system and thus treating your cough episodes. It also acts as an anti-inflammatory agent that kills bacteria and infection.

Broccoli in Spicy Sauce

Ingredients:

- 1 broccoli (cut into small florets)
- 2 teaspoon cornstarch mixed with 2 tablespoon water
- 4 garlic cloves (minced)
- 4-5 red chili (minced)
- 2 tablespoon vegan soy sauce
- ¼ cup water
- 2 tablespoon vegetable oil
- ! teaspoon salt
- 1 teaspoon pepper

Utensils Needed:

- Wok
- Spatula
- Kitchen knife
- Chopping board

Directions:

Cut the broccoli into small florets and mince the garlic and red chili. Now, heat 2 tablespoon of vegetable oil in a wok. Once oil is hot and shimmering, stir-fry garlic and red chili. Add broccoli florets into the wok and cook until stem is tender. Pour ¼ cup of water into the wok and add the cornstarch mixture. Mix all the ingredients and then bring to a simmer. When the sauce thickens, add 2 tablespoons of vegan soy sauce. Season with salt and pepper, then mix. Serve hot to 4-5 persons.

In cooking broccoli, you can immediately stir-fry it after washing with water. Just make sure to let it dry first before sautéing. You can also boil it in a pot of water with salt, and then drain water using a colander. Let it cool and dry for a couple of minutes, then proceed to sautéing.

Health Tips:
- If you don't want to have skin cancer, you should always protect yourself with sunscreen when expose to sunlight. Broccoli provides a natural sunscreen in preventing you from acquiring skin problems like skin cancer or sunburns. It contains Sulforaphane a natural compound that protects you from UV rays of the sun.

Garlic Mushroom with Vegan Soy Sauce and Vinegar

Ingredients:

- 500 grams Portobello or Button Mushrooms
- 7 cloves garlic (chopped)
- 1 bay leaf
- 2 tablespoon vegan soy sauce (tamari)
- 2 tablespoon rice vinegar or white vinegar
- Minced parsley for garnish
- 1 teaspoon white sugar
- 2 tablespoon vegetable oil
- 1 teaspoon pepper
- Salt to taste
- 4 tablespoon vegetable stock

Utensils Needed:

- Wok
- Spatula
- Chopping board
- Kitchen knife

Directions:

Prepare all your ingredients. Wash mushroom, parsley and garlic with water. Remove the husk of garlic and then chop into medium sizes.. Cut parsley into small pieces and save for garnish.

Heat 2 tablespoons of vegetable oil in a wok. Add garlic when oil is hot. Sauté until garlic turns brown. Add 500 grams of Portobello mushroom and stir-fry until tender. Pour 2 tablespoons of tamari sauce, 2 tablespoons of white vinegar and 4 tablespoons of vegetable stock into the wok. Mix to coat the mushrooms well. Sprinkle with a teaspoon of white cane sugar, pepper and salt to taste. Add 1 bay leaf and bring to simmer. Garnish with minced parsley and serve warm to 4-5

persons.

Health Tips:
- Portobello mushroom is pact with phosphorus that ensures healthy bone development. It also plays a role in removing waste products through the kidneys and prevent you from having muscle cramps.

Corn Soup

Ingredients:

- 1 can sweet corn kernels
- 1 medium size carrot (minced)
- 1 can almond milk
- 2 cups vegetable stock
- 1 cup water
- 1 tablespoon corn starch mixed with 3 tablespoon water
- 2 inches ginger (grated)
- 1 large onion (minced)
- 3 tablespoons chopped spring onions for garnish
- 1 teaspoon pepper
- 1 teaspoon salt

Utensils Needed:

- Pot
- Ladle
- Kitchen knife
- Chopping board
- Shredder

Directions:

Wash one medium size carrot, 2 inches ginger and one large onion with cold running water then remove the skin. Cut the carrot and onion into small pieces, then using a shredder, grate the ginger.

Place a pot on top of the stove and turn on medium heat. Pour a cup of water and 2 cups of vegetable stock into the pot. Add carrots, ginger and onion. Mix in 1 can of sweet corn kernels and stir the soup using a ladle. Add a cup of almond milk and cover the pot. Let it boil for 5-7 minutes and then slowly add the cornstarch mixture while continuously stirring. Sprinkle with a teaspoon of salt and pepper. When the soup thickens, garnish with chopped spring onions. Serve hot to 5 persons.

Health Tips:

- The belief that carrots can improve your vision started during World War II. A campaign ad during that time showed carrots could help military men see in the dark. Carrots contain beta-carotene and lutein; two substances that help improve your eyesight. Eating carrots can prevent you from getting any eye problems in the future.

Bamboo Shoot Adobo (cooked in Soy Sauce, Vinegar and Garlic)

Ingredients:

- 550 grams bamboo shoots (cut into strips about 2-3 inches long)
- 7 tablespoons vegan soy sauce
- 5 tablespoons white vinegar
- 8 garlic cloves (chopped)
- 1 bay leaf
- 1 teaspoon pepper
- 1 teaspoon salt
- 3 tablespoons vegetable oil
- 1 teaspoon honey

Utensils Needed:

- Frying pan
- Spatula
- Chopping board
- Kitchen knife
- Pot with water
- Colander

Directions:

Wash bamboo shoots with water and remove the hard outer layer. Cut off the root end and slice into strips. Now, boil a pot of water and add the strips of bamboo shoots. Cook for about an hour then drain the water using a colander. Pat the bamboo shoots with a clean cloth and let it cool in room temperature.

Prepare 8 cloves of garlic and chop into small pieces. In a wok, add 3 tablespoons of vegetable oil. Sauté the garlic when the oil is shimmering and hot. Add the strips of bamboo shoots and stir-fry until crisp. Pour 7 tablespoons of vegan soy sauce and 5 tablespoons of white vinegar into the wok. Mix everything to coat the bamboo shoots with the sauce. Add a teaspoon of honey and sprinkle with a teaspoon of salt and pepper. Cook for about 5-6 minutes. Stir frequently to avoid burning the bamboo shoots. Serve warm with rice to 5-6 persons.

Health Tips:
- Bamboo shoots can help heal wounds due to its anti-inflammatory properties. It can help cure gastric ulcers too.
- Honey can also treat gastric ulcers like bamboo shoots. It acts as an anti-bacterial agent in your gastrointestinal system. Having this two in one dish can really help you have a healthier tummy.

Cabbage Soup Filipino Style

Ingredients:

- 1 head cabbage (shredded)
- 1 large tomato (chopped)
- 1 large onion (sliced)
- 2 cups vegetable stock
- 2 tablespoon light soy sauce
- 2 teaspoon sugar
- 1 teaspoon salt
- 1 teaspoon pepper
- 2 inches ginger (grated)
- 4 cloves garlic (minced)
- 3 cups water
- 1 teaspoon cumin powder

Utensils Needed:

- Pot
- Shredder
- Kitchen knife
- Chopping board
- Ladle

Directions:

Rinse cabbage with water and remove any dried and yellowish outer leaves. Grate using a shredder and then set aside. Wash onion, ginger, garlic and tomato with cold water. Pat to dry and then remove the skin of onion, ginger and garlic. Chop all vegetables into small pieces, then save for later use.

Bring a pot of 3 cups water. Heat over medium flame. Add 2 cups of vegetable stock, then put onion, tomato, ginger and garlic into the pot. Cover the pot and let it simmer. Now, add the shredded cabbage and whisk using a ladle. Pour

2 tablespoons of light soy sauce and add a teaspoon of cumin powder. Cover the pot and bring to a boil. Stir occasionally while cooking the cabbage. Sprinkle a teaspoon of pepper and salt, then add 2 teaspoons of sugar into the pot. Mix everything well. Cook for another 2 minutes and then serve hot to 6 persons.

Health Tips:
- Cumin acts as a detoxifying agent in your body and helps you get rid of acne or pimples. If you want a smooth and healthy skin, you should mix some cumin powder in your recipes.

Cauliflower with Carrots in Thick Garlic Sauce

Ingredients:

- 1 large cauliflower (cut into florets)
- 1 large carrot (sliced diagonally)
- ¼ cup vegetable stock
- 2 teaspoon cornstarch mixed with 2 tablespoons water
- 2 tablespoon tamari sauce
- 1 teaspoon pepper
- 1 teaspoon salt
- 2 teaspoons white cane sugar
- 3 tablespoon olive oil
- 6 garlic cloves (minced)

Utensils Needed:

- Wok
- Spatula
- Kitchen knife
- Chopping board

Directions:

Wash cauliflower with salt and water. Let it soak for about 5 minutes to kill bugs and remove dirt. Cut the cauliflower into small florets and set aside. Wash garlic and carrot with water and remove the skin. Chop the carrot diagonally into 2 inches long and mince the garlic.

Now, place a skillet or wok on a stove over medium heat. Add 3 tablespoons of olive oil and let it shimmer. Once oil is hot, sauté garlic until golden. Add the cauliflower florets and sliced carrots into the wok. Stir-fry until vegetables are tender. Pour ¼ cup of vegetable stock into the wok and add cornstarch mixture. Season with salt, pepper, and sprinkle with 2 teaspoons of sugar. Cook until the sauce thicken. Stir occasionally. Serve warm with rice to 4-5 persons.

Health Tips:
- Sulforaphane in cauliflower helps maintain a normal DNA function. This substance can be found in cruciferous plants like cauliflower. Eating cauliflower provides you an improved metabolism due to its effect in your cells.

Mung Beans Coconut Popsicle

Ingredients:

- ½ cup coconut juice
- ½ cup coconut milk
- 1 ½ cup coconut cream
- ½ cup honey syrup
- ½ cup maple syrup
- 1 can sweetened mung beans
- 1 cup grated coconut

Utensils Needed:

- Popsicle mold
- Pot
- Metal whisker
- Blender
- Popsicle sticks
- Large mixing bowl
- Wooden spoon or spatula

Directions:

Put ½ cup of coconut milk and 1 ½ cup of coconut cream in a pot. Turn stove on low flame. Let it simmer and mix using a metal whisker until mixture becomes thick. Let it cool and save for later use.

In a blender, combine ½ cup of maple syrup, half cup of honey and ½ cup of coconut juice. Pulse until mixture turns smooth. Transfer to a large mixing bowl and pour the coconut cream mixture into the bowl. Now, toss all the ingredients carefully with a wooden spoon or spatula. Save for later use.

Get your Popsicle molds. Pour 1 can of sweetened mung beans equally on each mold. Mix grated coconut into the mold. Just make sure to cover just ¼ of the mold. Then transfer coconut mixture into each mold. Refrigerate for about 15-30 minutes and then put a Popsicle stick in each mold. Place it again in the refrigerator and chill overnight. Serve cold to 7-8 persons.

Health Tips:
- Maple syrup helps in maintaining a normal male reproductive system. It contains Zinc that helps prostate gland to function well. Adding maple syrup to your meals will keep you from having prostate cancer.

Sticky Rice Balls with Jack Fruit Recipe

Ingredients:

- 2 cups coconut milk
- 2 cups coconut cream
- 1 cup jack fruit
- ½ cup white cane sugar
- 3 tablespoons honey syrup
- 1 teaspoon vanilla syrup
- ½ cup sago pearls
- 1 cup sticky rice balls (1 cup stick rice flour mixed with ½ cup water)
- 5 cups water (for cooking sago pearls)

Utensils Needed:

- Pot
- Ladle
- Strainer or colander
- Large mixing bowl
- Wooden spatula

Directions:

Prepare 1 cup of sticky rice flour in a large mixing bowl. Add ½ cup of water and mix until mixture becomes stiff. Knead to make small rice balls. Save for later use.

Cook sago pearls in a pot of boiling water until it turns transparent. Drain water using a colander and set aside.

Combine 2 cups of coconut milk and 2 cups of coconut cream in a pot. Heat over medium flame. Add 1 cup of jackfruit, ½ cup of cooked sago pearls and 1 cup of prepared sticky rice balls. Stir using a ladle and cover the pot. Cook until rice balls float on the surface of the coconut mixture. Stir frequently to avoid rice balls sticking at the bottom of the pot. Dissolve ½ cup of sugar and pour 3 tablespoons of honey and a teaspoon of vanilla into the pot. Mix all the ingredients and bring to a simmer. Serve warm to 6 persons.

Health Tips:
- Sago pearls come from the starchy trunk of Sago Palms. It is commonly mixed with milk in Asian countries like the Philippines. Sago pearl is low in fat and calories. It is considered a light food and is easy to digest.

Potato Chips Filipino Recipe

Ingredients:

- 6 pieces large potatoes (thinly sliced)
- 6 cups water
- 1 tablespoon salt
- Vegetable oil for deep frying
- Chili powder (optional)

Utensils Needed:

- Large skillet
- Strainer
- Kitchen knife
- Large bowl
- Chopping board

Directions:

Wash potatoes with water and peel the skin. Cut potatoes into thin slices and then soak in a bowl of water. Add a tablespoon of salt and let it stand for about 3 hours. Drain water and pat to dry using a clean cloth.

Prepare a large skillet with vegetable oil, about 3-4 cups. Heat the oil over medium flame. Now, add the sliced potatoes and deep-fry until golden. Strain excess oil and transfer to a plate topped with a paper towel. You can sprinkle chili powder on top of the potatoes to give it a spicy taste. Serving is about 6-8 person.

Health Tips:

- Potatoes are full of anti-oxidants that can help

you fight free radicals. Eating potatoes like French fries or potato chips can prevent you from having cancer cells. Just make sure to cook homemade chips and fries and don't just buy the ready-made in the groceries.

Steamed Brown Rice Cake with Grated Coconut

Ingredients:

- 1 ½ cup rice flour
- 2 teaspoon lye water
- 1 tablespoon annatto seeds (mixed with 3 tablespoon water)
- ½ cup all-purpose flour or tapioca flour
- 3 cups water
- ¼ cup white sugar
- ¾ cups brown sugar

Utensils Needed:

- Steamer
- Molds
- Large mixing bowl
- Wooden spoon or spatula
- Strainer

Directions:

Prepare annatto seeds mixture. Add 3 tablespoons of water in a small bowl and mix with 1 tablespoon of annatto seeds. Let it soak for about an hour, and then drain the seeds. Save annatto water for later use.

Combine rice flour, tapioca or all-purpose flour, brown and white sugar and 3 cups of water in a large mixing bowl. Stir mixture using a wooden spatula. Mix well. Gradually add 2 teaspoons of lye water and annatto water in the rice mixture. Now, transfer the rice cake mixture into small cupcake molds. Place in a steamer and steam for an hour. Let it cool and then remove the rice cake out of the molds. Serve to 5-6 persons with grated coconut on top.

Health Tips:
- As you age, your bones become brittle and soft. Ample amounts of Calcium is needed by your bones to stay strong and healthy. Annatto seeds are packed with Calcium that can enhance your bone strength and will prevent you from acquiring bone diseases, as you get older.

Made in the USA
Monee, IL
14 May 2023